# TRANSCENDING

## REFLECTIONS OF CRIME VICTIMS

# TRANSCENDING

## REFLECTIONS OF CRIME VICTIMS

portraits and interviews by
HOWARD ZEHR

Good Books

Intercourse, PA 17534
800/762-7171
www.goodbks.com

Design by Dawn J. Ranck

TRANSCENDING: REFLECTIONS OF CRIME VICTIMS
Copyright © 2001 by Good Books, PO Box 419, Intercourse, PA 17534
\International Standard Book Number: 1-56148-337-0 (hardcover)
International Standard Book Number: 1-56148-333-8 (paperback)
Library of Congress Catalog Card Number: 2001033226

Library of Congress Cataloging-in-Publication Data

Zehr, Howard
   Transcending : reflections of crime victims : portraits and interviews / by Howrd Zehr.
     p. cm.
   ISBN: 1-56148-337-0 (hardcover) — ISBN: 1-56148-333-8 (paperback)
   1. Victims of crimes--United States--Psychology--Case studies. 2. Victims of violent crimes--United States--Psychology--Case studies. 3. Violent crimes--United States--Psychological aspects--Case studies. I. Title.

HV6250.3.U5 Z44 2001
362.88 0973--dc21                                        2001033226

# Table of Contents

# *About This Book*

## Howard Zehr

The heart of this book consists of reflections—words and portraits—of women and men who have undergone our worst nightmares. These survivors of violent crime speak of tragedy and trauma, but they don't stop there. They go on to describe and reflect on their journeys to work through these experiences and to build new lives. While all characterize the path as painful and ongoing, some say they have found peace. Although some object to being called strong, most have discovered new sources of strength. Even though the coherence of their lives was disrupted or destroyed, many have found new levels of meaning. This is a book of paradoxes and surprises. Given our stereotypes of victims, it may not be the book you expect.

The words we typically use to describe such experiences and processes are problematic. Do you *recover* or *rebuild* after a violent attack or the loss of a loved one? Lynn Shiner (page 8) doesn't think so. Do you *heal*? Certainly you don't find *closure*—Emma Jo Snyder (page 38) and others will attest to that. The persons who speak here choose metaphors instead—puzzles, maps, chain links, Burma Shave signs, a stone, a rose.

With some trepidation, I have settled on the word *transcending* as the focus of this book, even though it isn't a term commonly used in the field of victimology. The definition in *Merriam Webster's Collegiate Dictionary, Tenth Edition,* captures some important themes of the witnesses represented in this book: rising above or going beyond the limits, triumphing over negative or restrictive aspects, extending notably beyond ordinary limits.

Vaclav Havel, formerly a dissident under the Czechoslovakian communist regime, later president of the Czech Republic, stated the options as he saw them: "Transcendence is the only alternative to extinction."

Here, then, are the words and visages of women and men who have faced the abyss and have transcended, are in the process of transcending, or are searching for toeholds on the climb to transcendence. In Part I of this book they offer their reflections.

In Part II, I offer my own. Here I present my attempt to understand victimization and what justice owes victims, exploring these questions: Why is violent crime so traumatic? What passage must victims make in order to cope with and perhaps transcend the experience? What part can justice play in that process? In Part II I seek to provide a conceptual and analytical framework based on victims' realities.

## Our Own Fears Unnerve Us

My goal in this project is to enable all of us—ordinary citizens, justice professionals, change advocates—to better understand the experiences, the perspectives, the needs of crime victims. Indeed, our internal defensive mechanisms help screen us from facing these traumatic possibilities. Due to what we might call vicarious victimization when we hear about others' experiences of violence, we become vulnerable to similar feelings. To avoid this vulnerability, we often don't allow ourselves to hear. And we blame victims for what happened to them: it was their fault; I wouldn't do that, so I am safe. I'd like this book to catch readers off-guard, breaking through these defenses and stereotypes, encouraging us to understand and to accept what we do not understand.

## "Hand Down a Rope to Others"

My hope has also been that this book might, as Susan Russell (page 64) puts it, hand down a rope to others who have experienced such tragedies and traumas. Ideally, those who are at different places in the process might find in the reflections of others some clues, some hope. At the same time, if you are in such a situation, I would urge you to resist the temptation to measure yourself against those in this book. Every journey is different, and, while the voices here may contain clues and ideas, they certainly do not offer a road map or common destination. I do not intend this to be a collection of preachments or prescriptions. I do hope that by focusing on transcendence, the trauma of violence is not minimized. Indeed, the pain is very real and very important to acknowledge and understand.

I am not totally comfortable with everything that persons in this book say, and you may not be either. But these are their experiences, their views, and they need to be heard. I work in the field of restorative justice (more on that in Part II, "Looking for the Burma Shave Signs; Victimization and the Obligations of Justice," beginning on page 185). A foundational principle of restorative justice is that the process of justice must be victim-centered. This means that victims' voices must be heard and that victims' needs—as they define them—must be addressed. Victims should have a right and a place to say what they need to say. As Bion Dolman (page 142) testifies so eloquently, that opportunity is rarely provided to victims, even in the justice process. This book is an effort to provide such a space, without censure.

## A Choir

I have, of course, excerpted these stories from interviews that ran from one to four hours. That inevitably involves a selection process. However, while I have sometimes changed the order of what was said and have made a few additions for clarity or transition, these are their words. But they are not all of their words. I have conceived this book as a dramatic reading or a choir with many voices and roles. Each selection is one voice contributing to the choir of witnesses. Common themes were expressed by many persons, although I have not always recorded them here. I have tried to include those distinctive aspects of each story that seemed especially crucial to a person's experience and/or identity.

Even though many of the people featured in this book are at some distance from the experience of violence, I must emphasize that their views do not remain static; understandings and interpretations are always in flux. So keep in mind that each of the selections in this book reflect one moment in time, a particular point on a journey, and may not fully represent where that person is now. This is apparent in the several selections where I do include updates.

## Who Are These People?

In selecting people to interview and in editing, I wanted to incorporate the diversity, the complexity, the ambiguities, and contradictions that are characteristic of victims' experiences. At the same time, the book is not a fully representative sample by gender, ethnicity, or geography (although the interview sites did range over a wide area). People of color are under-represented compared to the incidence of their victimization, as are inner-city residents. Women and homicide survivors are over-represented. This may have occurred in part because my referral sources were largely victim service agencies and a few restorative justice programs. I suspect that some groups of people are more likely than others to use these services and to maintain contact with them over time.

When soliciting referrals, I asked only that the individuals had gone through some form of severe criminal violence, that they were at least a few years away from the trauma, and that they would be willing to reflect on what happened. I did not ask that they have any particular views or experiences.

Although I had certain matters that I hoped to explore, my approach was open-ended and conversational. After asking them whether they could briefly tell me what happened, I usually asked, "How do you go on, how do you put a life together, after something like that?" Another early question was, "What are the main issues or questions you've had to deal with?" We went on from there to talk about stages and turning points, about language, rituals, and metaphors, about justice and faith.

The question of forgiveness often came up. I was particularly interested in the disruption and reordering of meaning in trauma and transcendence, so we usually talked about that. The only stock questions I asked were at the end: "How are you different because of this?" "How is 'normal' different?" "Has any good come of this?" "What have you learned about the meaning of life?" often made them laugh or groan.

For me the conversations were moving, inspiring, astonishing, but also difficult. As the project progressed, I found myself becoming increasingly emotional, sometimes tearing up during the interviews, even when my interview partner did not. After the interviews, I often thought about these people and their experiences; I was moved to contemplate issues of life, meaning, and faith in new ways. I needed space at times, but I never wanted to quit. I certainly received a great deal, for which I am grateful.

## The Responsibilities of an Interviewer

The persons whose stories are in this book have been through extreme experiences that have shaken them to the core. Some have not gone public with what they've undergone before this. Their being willing to let a stranger into their lives, to share with such depth and intimacy, to offer such trust, has been both a gift to me, as well as my awesome responsibility. My friend Ingrid DeSanctis tells her drama students, "It is a sacred trust to represent someone." Indeed it is. I have tried hard not to violate that trust.

When I teach research, I stress to students that when they undertake an interview project, they have formed a kind of partnership with their subject. I remind them that they have obligations to their partners, that they must be accountable to them in some way, and that part of their responsibility is to give something back whenever possible. Throughout this project, I have tried here to live up to those principles: by designing the project with the interests of survivors in mind, by offering photos and transcripts to participants, by editing with integrity, by soliciting feedback from those interviewed about their selections, and by having a number of victims and victim advocates read and make suggestions about the manuscript.

These are the voices and images of the people I interviewed, but I must admit that they have been shaped by my vision as well. As the literature of qualitative research says, knowledge gained through interviews is always mutually constructed through the interaction of all who participate in the dialogue. It would be a delusion to claim that these are purely the interviewees' voices, uninfluenced by our interaction or the editing process.

By providing a safe environment to respond to reflective questions, I hope that the interviews themselves, or the opportunity to read their own interviews later, will allow people to gain new insights about their experiences or to put things together in a new way. I am thankful that this seems to have happened for many of the participants. Joseph Baratta, at the end of his interview, comments that "it's been a mercy and a help to be able to talk about this after all these years." Penny Beerntsen wrote, after seeing her edited selection, "Transcendence is ongoing, and this project has moved me to a new and better place!" When I sent Debra Franke her selection for response, I got this email: "I've read 'my story' several times this evening. The first time was through a veil of tears. Yes, the pain is always there . . . The second and third reading reminded me of all the good parts of my life and my wonderful relationship with my loving mother." I am glad when this work can serve as a record and a reminder as well.

I have used the language of research here, but I am most comfortable seeing myself within the documentary tradition. Documentary workers have a long practice of combining photographs and words in an attempt to give voice and identity to people and their experiences. They have also recognized that this enterprise is a subjective process influenced by their own history and outlook, that it involves art and intuition as much as science. In his book, **Doing Documentary Work**, Robert Coles summarizes it like this:

> . . . doing documentary work is a journey, and is a little more, too, a passage across boundaries (disciplines, occupational constraints, definitions, conventions all too influentially closed for traffic), a passage that can become a quest, even a pilgrimage, a movement toward the sacred truth enshrined not only on tablets of stone, but in the living hearts of those whom we can hear, see, and get to understand. Thereby, we hope to be confirmed in our own humanity—the creature on this earth whose very nature it is to make just that kind of connection with others during the brief stay we are permitted here (p. 145).

For me, documentary work such as this book is a means to help people share themselves, a form that seeks to bridge the chasms that separate people. One artist said, "Artists are supposed to be on the cutting edge. I want to be on the healing edge." That image has nourished me through this book: to work, not on the cutting edge, but on the healing edge.

# Part I

# Stories and Reflections
# of Crime Victims

# "All the rungs on a ladder are removed."

My ex-husband Tom had chosen not to see Jennifer and David at all from January to September, 1994. Then in September, out of the blue, he started wanting to be part of their lives. Something changed, and I thought it was positive. Christmas Eve day he picked them up, and he was probably in the best mood I had ever seen him be in. The next morning we found that he had stabbed Jen and Dave, then killed himself.

Little did I know, until after it all happened, that he had an actual checklist of everything he needed to do. The last item was to kill Jennifer and David. He thought David was the devil and Jennifer was an angel. We found out later that he thought he was God and that he was doing some kind of wonderful thing by saving them from this life.

The only constant I had after that was my job. I didn't have Jen and Dave. I couldn't bear to stay over or sleep in my home, so I lost my house. Friends that I thought I had weren't friends. It was like starting at zero.

I had constant panic attacks and I really struggled with suicide. I replayed things—my ritual was to get in the tub every night and play everything over and over again. I put myself in Jennifer's position. I put myself in David's. Jennifer was killed first and didn't know what happened. The hardest thing was what David was feeling at that moment; how could any father do something like that? The what-ifs were just endless for me. The visions and memories overwhelmed me because nothing made sense.

People didn't know what to do so they avoided me. People thought that if they'd bring up the subject, they'd hurt me, so our relationships just faded. I needed people who were associated with Jen and Dave. But as time goes on, sometimes I feel that that group of friends expects me to stay sad; they don't want me to move on. I think I'm disconnecting with them.

LYNN SHINER

*I can't reorder anything because if I did, I would just pick up the scrambled pieces and put them back in order. It's more like all the rungs on a ladder are removed. I'm at the bottom and have to start all over. You build, you create a new life. I have a couple of pieces from my old life that I have fit in.*

I enjoy company with my friend Carol and others who never knew Jen and Dave. It helps that she has victim experience, and she just takes me for who I am. I can just be me, and it's okay that I want to enjoy life. When I see Carol, there's no association with Jen and Dave. Now I don't need somebody to generate memories because they are inside me—Jen and Dave are here right now. They are constantly with me.

Now I don't need to dwell on what happened. No matter how many what-ifs, I can't bring them back. In my mind I have a china cabinet with glass doors and there's a key to it. Fairly often I open my china cabinet, and I take out Jen and Dave. I go through what happened to Jen and Dave, but in order to be okay I put them back in. I put them away and close the door, but I'm only closing the door on that tiny part, the murder. I have such good memories and I have a presence of them here. They are here, they're with me, and they leave me signs all the time.

In the beginning, I felt I had no right to be happy. That was a major struggle. How can I be happy when I don't have Jen and David? Now I can say that I'm happy, although I'm not as happy as I could be. I know I go down a lot, but not as often. When I go down, sometimes I can't explain it and sometimes it's because of a trigger. At Christmas I go down severely. I don't celebrate Christmas at all.

I don't think I'd be here without my present husband Paul. Anytime I had thoughts of suicide, he always wanted me to tell him. Instead of being angry at me he'd say, "Just talk about it." Sometimes talking and putting those thoughts out there made me feel better. He was a real pillar. And staying busy was important. I started running with my husband and we trained for a marathon. By the end of the day, I'd be completely wiped out. I think I took a lot of frustration and anger out that way. I read a lot, too; it helped me to know that I was not crazy. And I never had a pet before, but this guy—this cat—made a huge difference in the grieving process. Animals know when you don't feel well and just come up and cuddle on your chest.

In my dreams I've killed Tom a good two dozen times in some of the grossest, most gruesome ways you can imagine. I've tortured him to no end. Then I'd wake up very upset. You don't think you're capable of killing, but in those dreams, the trigger clicks so easily! I know they're just dreams. That's not me. I don't think

I would hurt anybody, but how do you know until you go through it?

I'm not totally in control yet, but I decided that I didn't want to just exist. I value life, and for Jen and Dave to be so shortchanged in life, I'm going to make up for them. It's like the three of us are in the routine together. They're with me, and it would be wrong for me not to value life. What would they think of me if I didn't value my own life? I need to make up for what they would have offered. I'm not going to fix or change the world, but, while I'm here, I'm going to make a difference. They're with me, and they're proud of me!

Do you know some of the things I've done? The first was to start a golf tournament in memory of Jen and Dave, and now we also have a silent auction. This year we expect to raise $50,000, and all the proceeds go to domestic violence programs.

After Tom killed Jen and Dave, I learned he had been stalking a disc jockey in Lancaster. She had called the police and written two letters saying that she was afraid for his children, and that the mother should be contacted. My first question was, "Why wasn't I ever notified?" That's how the Jen and Dave Law came about. The law is passed now and says that if two people are in a custody situation, each has the right to find out about the other person's criminal activity. I was appointed by the governor to the Victim Service Advisory Committee, and I now manage the Compensation Division.

*Redbook* did an article and asked me why I do these things. My response back then was because I'm selfish. If it benefits other people, fine, but that's an extra. Now, as time goes by, I'm starting to feel differently. It's not just for me anymore.

I'm different now. I feel that I have an advantage over my old self. When I said "Don't sweat the small stuff" before, I was just saying it. Now I have it in my heart. So many things don't mean anything to me anymore. I have lots to keep me busy, but I'm not in a real hurry anymore. And I have people skills that just came out of somewhere. I don't know if they were always there, but now I don't just deal with the task, I deal with the person.

I joke with a friend of mine that I know I need to forgive, so when I'm on my deathbed and there's only five second left, then I'll forgive him. There's surely no need now. What's the purpose? God tells you that you need to forgive, so I'll just sneak that in right at the end.

*Eighteen months later:* Through recent experiences, I've come to realize the darkness and anger that are still in my head, and the amount of energy they take from me. He has ruined my past. I'm beginning to toy with the idea of forgiveness so that I don't allow him to destroy my future as well.

— Lynn Shiner

# "For so many years, nobody believed me."

When I was 11 years old, I said to my grandmother, "Why does life hurt so much?" She said, "I don't know, baby, but remember this: all of us are here for a reason. Some of us have to hurt before we find our reason." Since my face-to-face meeting with my stepfather, my abuser, I've come to believe that one reason I was abused, the reason I was called a mouthy little bitch, was so that I would know what pain is like. I think my purpose now is to stop others from going through it. If I'm still a mouthy bitch, so be it. But I'm going to let people know abuse can happen in your own backyard.

Mental and physical abuse is what I grew up with from the day I was born. My father was alcoholic and brutally violent. My aunt remembers one time when she had to go get the police because he had a gun to my head and was threatening to blow my head off. Eventually my mother left him and became an alcoholic, and

I became in charge of my sister and me. Then my mother met my stepdad. He made her stop beating us but then the sexual abuse started. It carried on until I got married at 19 and left home.

Then my first husband was also alcoholic and abused me; he raped me with a broken beer bottle in the middle of the night. My mother and my sister refused to speak to me for two years when I left my first husband because they didn't believe what I told them about him.

For so many years, no one believed me about the sexual abuse because my stepfather told everyone I was a lying little bitch, that I was the one causing trouble. Even Social Services didn't do anything, and the police said, "There is nothing we can do since your mother refuses to press charges and you are under age." That's when I gave up on the justice system. It was like a slap in the face. Later, my second husband encouraged me to press charges and I did, but

JANET BAKKE

*Everyone talks about steps to healing, steps to closure. For me it's more like chapters. This chapter is over—it's time to move on to the next one.*

my biggest regret in life was going to trial. I lost too much; it wasn't worth it.

When I was young, I almost turned to prostitution because it was a way of not having to go home. But something inside me just said, No. I never did drugs, I never drank, I never did prostitution. I always tried to stay on the good side, because deep inside I knew that one day the people that hurt me were going to pay. I wanted to make sure that when I made them pay, I could stand up and defend myself with a clear conscience. I didn't want to give them the excuse that, "Oh, she doesn't remember because she was on drugs." In a way, they all have paid, although not enough. Grandma said that in the end, those who do wrong will pay, and those who do right will not. I know that when they meet their maker, they are not going to meet the same maker as I am!

There were no high points in my life before my son was born in 1986. He was my first accomplishment, in my books. Another high point for me was meeting Dave and Sandy from the victim offender mediation program. They believed in me. They didn't pity me but they understood, and they never said it didn't happen. That was what I had been searching for—somebody just to believe me, because nobody would.

Then they gave me something I had wanted all my life: a chance to sit down with my stepfather and question him without him being able to get up and run away. To hear him actually admit the truth was one of the highest points of my life. It was the first time he actual-

ly admitted that he had done those things. It was the first time he didn't call me a lying little bitch.

It was a healing stage because I needed to tell him how he destroyed my life. I was able to face him, and I wasn't afraid of him anymore. I got to hold him accountable to *me*—not to the justice system, not to his case management officer. He had to sit there and look me in the eye and be accountable to me. He had control over me all those years; now I took control.

You know what? It was a better feeling than if you handed me a check for a million dollars. And when he said, "You didn't put me here; I put myself here," it was the most powerful thing he could have said, because he finally admitted it. I don't believe he fully believed those words—they were out of a book—but it was helpful because I had witnesses when he said, "I did this to you."

I'm not angry with him anymore. I told him at the face-to-face that I forgave him because I know deep in my heart that he didn't do it to hurt me. He did it because that was the only thing he knew. Also, my relationship with him wasn't all bad either. He taught me a lot of good. But he's not ready to be in society. I put him in jail so he could learn appropriate behavior, but he's not learning it. He's going to do it again. What a waste of time!

The meeting with my stepfather in prison was the end of a chapter, the end of my being angry with him. The next chapter was grief. I had to come to terms with the fact that I had lost my stepfather forever and that he's not going to change.

Ten years ago I hated the world and thought the world owed me. I hated my mother, my sister, my father. I don't hate any of them anymore. Sometimes I'm angry with them and I feel sorry for them, but I don't hate them like I used to. I know, too, that I'm never going to get what I want out of the world. I can only get what I want from *me*. I'm the one who will change things. Nobody else can do it for me.

The dove has become my own little symbol because of my search for peace, but also because it is a sign of freedom. As a child, I thought I was searching for freedom, but it wasn't freedom. It was peace. I confused it with freedom because my stepdad and mom had such control over me. I realized about six months ago that I had to make peace with myself and forgive myself before I could expect others to make peace with me. My life has been a big storm and now it's calm.

— Janet Bakke

# "I have to live with the fact that I made that decision."

My son had been incarcerated in the county jail on a drug charge. One day my assistant came into my office and said, "Your son is in the reception unit here." I went down, and there he was. He said, "Before you say anything, Dad, I'm sorry."

Since I'm the superintendent of this prison, I said, "You know I can't keep you here," and I made arrangements to send him back to the county jail. That's the last time I saw my son alive. He was killed there in an argument over a robe that I had purchased for him.

Maybe if he had gone somewhere upstate he would be out today. I've walked around with that guilt. I have to live with the fact that I made that decision, but I have to make decisions all the time. I am in charge of 1,000 staff and 4,259 inmates at any given time. You use your best judgment, your training, your knowledge. You never know what the real outcome is

going to be. I thought I was doing the right thing by not keeping him here. If I had sent him to Camp Hill prison, it could have happened there.

My son was headed down the wrong path, but it didn't have to come to this. Inmates wrote me later that it shouldn't have happened, that the staff turned their backs because they were scared of the perpetrator. It was negligence that caused my son to be where he was inside the jail. At the trial, it came out that some persons in key positions tried to cover certain this up. I was bitter and sort of angry, but at the same time I'm part of the system.

There's not a day that I don't think about my son. I took his picture down because I feel that it's time to move on. I can't continue to live in the past, but I still have a card here that he gave to me that says, "Dad." He'll always be here.

As I looked at Brooks, the perpetrator, during the trial, I had hatred for him. But near the end

**DONALD VAUGHN**

*I got all kinds of condolences from inmates, cards made by inmates. As I walked through the jail, inmates told me they would have looked out for my son. I knew I was part of this community. That's what helped me through. And I knew then that I could not hold what happened against other inmates.*

of the trial, I began to see that he was a sick individual. His way of life and his thinking were warped. He's a victim of circumstances, a sick environment. I don't see him as an individual I feel any malice for. Revenge is not the answer. If I were to continually hate him, he would have won because he would have brought me to the position that he's in. I won't allow that.

If we want our children to be followers of uprighteousness, to believe in God and doing the right thing, then we have to give up hating. I have to be able to say that I can forgive. I wouldn't let the guy out of prison, but I don't hate him.

Not too long ago Brooks' file came across my desk. He was coming here to this prison to go to court. I said, "No." The reason I didn't want him here is because if something happened to him, they'd blame me. And I don't want to be the cause of anything happening to him.

Without the Lord I would not have been able to make it through. Every once in awhile I have to have some time alone to talk to the Lord about what has occurred here. And sometimes I cry about this. Some people think there's weakness in a man that cries. But if I don't cry, it'll build up inside of me. I have to get it off. And I talk to the Lord. Sometimes it doesn't do any good to talk to man because man bounces things right back on you.

Every day when I get into my car to come to work, I pray, "Thank the Lord." I have a thing about hugging my wife when I leave. You know why? Because I may not return.

— Donald Vaughn

*If we want our children*
*to be followers of uprighteousness,*
*to believe in God*
*and doing the right thing,*
*then we have to give up hating.*

# "We were not only responsible for our own grief, but for the community's."

I found when the girls died, everything was peeled away and I had no excuses. I'm stripped down to the bare bones and yet I sense that in this tragedy, I've been given an opportunity. Great, now I've got to feel good about this. Oh, shit, I've lost everything and now I've got to feel fucking good about it—pardon the language.

I was the mother of two teenage daughters, 17 and 15. On December 6, 1991, my older daughter dropped her sister and a friend at the mall and went to work at a yogurt shop a couple of blocks away. At 11:03 p.m. police in a cruiser saw smoke coming from the yogurt shop. A few minutes later they discovered four bodies. Four girls, including my two daughters, had been shot in the head. They were nude and tied up and burned beyond recognition.

The whole city stopped. Everyone was stunned. How did it happen? When the police weren't finding anybody, that just added to the chaos. We who had lost our daughters found that we were not only responsible for our own grief, but for the grief of the community. That's just not fair, but it's the truth. We were responsible for everyone else feeling okay about this. We had to make them comfortable. And we had to allow them to nurture us when we really damn well didn't want to be nurtured. We wanted to be left the hell alone. We had to make sure that everyone else had a place to grieve, and it seemed to be our doorsteps. The murders were so public, and they hurt people at such a deep level that they came and came and came.

I know that what we had was a blessing and a curse in the same bag. How could I get through something like this? It was all those idiot people that were driving me nuts. I know that they were a blessing. It was awful, but they were a blessing. But we had too many, and we had tragedy groupies.

BARBARA AYRES

*At first, grief is so heavy and dark that you just want to get away from it. Then you understand that the grief is not ever leaving you. Finally, you've carried it so long that you don't notice it. You are like one of those ladies from Africa with the pots on her head: she carries a massive pot so well that she doesn't even notice it anymore.*

Now, after eight years, arrests were just made a few months ago. We're back in the public eye again—not that we have ever really been out of it. It's such a mixed bag. You want those people caught. You keep thinking, "If they don't find them, they are going to do this to somebody else." Plus you owe it to your children not to just act like it didn't happen, and to make sure there are consequences. And we need to know what happened. We have to know what we could have done differently as employers and as a community. On a real personal level, we need to know what we could have done differently as parents.

All those what-ifs. At first I said, "Shit, I should've gone earlier to pick them up, I should've, I should've . . ." But it's just too big. I had to let it go because it was out of my hands. Whoever did that was evil. You can't own that stuff. I've got lots of human qualities and frailties, but evil is not one of them. I make lots of mistakes, but I am not evil. I just stood up against that and said, "No!"

For a year, I sat on the edge of a couch. I didn't care if I ever started over. People were always bringing food—I think we had two years of lasagna in the freezer—but I didn't care if I ever ate again. Then I remembered a teacher in high school who told a story about a friend whose husband had died. When asked how she had recovered, she said, "I got up every day and took a bath and dressed." I remembered that so I made sure I took my bath. Let me tell you, it was hard to do those things we do so subconsciously. But you focus small and that's how you get through. It's incredible how small you have to get to recover.

All those crazy people came to see me, and, every once and awhile, somebody would say something right. Somebody said to me, "You shouldn't have any regrets. You did everything you could for your children while they were here." I took that one and held it. Sure, I have a few regrets, but mostly I don't. I wasn't perfect, but I wasn't terrible. When people spout out this crap to you, listen and get the good ones. Throw the rest away as quickly as possible.

You know you're supposed to learn something from this. Who knows where that voice comes from? Is that God? Is it Jennifer and Sarah? Is it your mother? Okay, what is it? You try so hard to put this in order, to make sense of it, and it won't let you. It's not sensible. I don't think life is nearly as philosophical as we would like to believe it is.

I felt very close to God when the girls died. I felt that I gave them back to God. I didn't say I wasn't pissed! Those aren't mutually exclusive. I was able to scream at God, "Why in the hell did you have to take both of them?" I got over it because the other side of it is that if he hadn't taken both of them, which one was going to stay? They were very close, and I couldn't bear to look at one of their faces without the other one. So as much as I whined about not having one of them, the blessing is that I don't have to look at one of those lonely faces. So I felt that I gave them back to God.

My girls are here with me all the time. I can still see them roll their eyes when I do something stupid. And they visit me occasionally in dreams. I usually get something from them: a lit- tle tidbit that will get me through the next cou- ple of few days. Whatever the question is, I get something from them that will help me get through. So if I ever write a book, it's going to be called *God Comes at 4:00 a.m.* There is a God, I swear there is. He will help you find your way, but you gotta look for it. You have to scratch it out, but he'll help you.

It has taken me a long time, but I think it is important for people to know that I'm happy. That's a hard thing to say, but I'm happy. I am at peace.

— Barbara Ayres

*"There's nothing like murder
to make you really, really look at yourself."*

# "What happened to the road map for living the rest of my life?"

I was considered for a position on the Board of Pardons because they decided they were going to have a victim on it. I told them this one experience is putting a label on me, like I was coming into the office with one of those "Hello, I'm a victim" stickers on my shirt. I said, "Let's pull this off right away. My name is Deb and I'm an army brat and I have two brothers. I went to Penn State. I have a career and a loving husband. We have a dog named Bernie. My mother was murdered. I ride a bicycle." We're more defined by all the rest of the experiences of our lives. That one experience is just part of it.

It was about 10 years ago that my mother stopped at the grocery store in a shopping center on her way home from work. From what we can tell, she was chosen at random because she presented a target of opportunity to Daniel. He overpowered her and took her and her car. At some point he stabbed her to death and put her body in the trunk where she bled to death. Later he burned her body.

The story doesn't end with her murder, and it didn't end with his apprehension. It didn't end with his confession or all the stuff that led up to him pleading guilty to first degree murder or when he tried to have that overturned. It never ends.

In the beginning there was shattering, howling pain. I functioned pretty well when there was a lot of structure, but if you took away the structure, I didn't do so well. Up until the time he was convicted and sentenced, I was just surviving each day to get to that point. I had a goal. But after things were settled and decided, I lost my focus. What happened to the road map for living the rest of my life? When he pled guilty, I lost a bit of that structure and I was left with just the rest of my life. It was up to me to deal with everything.

I had a videotape in my head, an image of a huge ball of pain. There were times that I just couldn't handle it, so I developed a mental

**DEBRA FRANKE**

*Because I'm so darn stubborn, I'm not going to let someone else control me. If I had let what he did that one day change everything about my philosophy of life, that would be saying, "You're in charge of my life." Bullshit—I'm in charge!*

image that I would put the pain in a box and say, "I'm not dealing with you right now." Sometimes I would make a conscious decision that, "Yep, now I'm going to think about this." I guess I still have that box, because there are times when I choose to think about what happened, choose to play the videotape. Then other times, I put it away.

I've tried hard to make sure that this one event, damn it, does not shape the rest of my life. My mother and I had 30-plus years of wonderful, positive experiences together. Part of getting on with life is not letting this one event, that had nothing to do with her and how she lived life, have an overwhelming negative effect on me. It is about making sure that her life isn't defined by that horrible event. So we had a memorial service that was somewhere between a religious service and a wake. Some played her favorite music on the harp. Others shared funny stories. That memorial service was really important from the standpoint of refusing to let Daniel Barnett define her life and not letting him have the last word.

I feel I'm responsible for my life and, if there's something I don't like about my life, I'm responsible to do something about it. So being able to integrate this as one terrible experience among millions of good experiences probably has a lot to do with the fact that I've got a can-do attitude about my whole life. Partly that is what my mother raised me to be.

I still cry. My mother's murder is not the defining event of my life now, but it is truly very painful. The howling pain is gone, but the pain itself isn't. I don't expect it ever to be gone. I wish I could say that this had no effect on me and my emotions and how I live my life. It has, but I work real hard at making sure it doesn't assume so high a level of significance that the bitterness overtakes the kind of person I want to be.

People have always said I see things through rose-colored glasses. Well, damn it, I wasn't going to take the rose-colored glasses off, just because someone did something so hurtful and horrible. I still assume people are fundamentally good, but now with this little seed of doubt. I always knew that bad things could happen. Well, now do I know bad things can happen! So I'm fundamentally the same person, but with this additional gut-level understanding: while life is good and the world is generally filled with good people, there are really bad people and bad things do happen.

— Debra Franke

*I've tried to make sure*
*that this one event does not shape the rest of my life.*
*I work real hard*
*at making sure it doesn't assume*
*so high a level of significance*
*that the bitterness overtakes the kind of person I want to be.*

# "You're getting all this support, and one day it's over."

*Robert:* Victim Services arrived at our home early in the morning of December 7, 1991. They told us that there had been a fire at the yogurt shop, and that our 13-year-old daughter Amy and three other girls had been killed. They weren't telling us a lot; they weren't truthful the whole time. Later we told them, "When something like this happens, I'm already in shock, so go ahead and tell me the truth. It makes it a whole lot easier. And don't say she was sexually assaulted. She was raped. The girls didn't just die in the yogurt shop. They were murdered." That's the way I want it—I don't want sugar coating.

The community went through this with us. In the funeral procession, there was a motorcycle cop that had to come to my house to ask me something about the case. I'm telling you, this man hurt with me. He broke down and just boohooed. Also, it's amazing the people you know who have already gone through something like this but had never let it surface before.

*Pam:* But then it works the other way. People who have been around you for a long time all of a sudden aren't comfortable with you. They don't know what to say. They don't know how to act around you. They don't realize that even though they might mention Amy and we might cry, it's still good. Because if they don't mention her, it's like she never existed.

*Robert:* People were supporting us, but one day it ended, and I was lost. You're getting all this support, and one day it's over. That's when you start to dig a hole.

*Pam:* At first, getting out of bed in the morning is a big deal. There's lots of mornings you think, "If I could just lie here and go back to sleep, I wouldn't have to deal with it." But you can't because you will wither up and die. So we made up our minds that we were going to try to be just as normal as we could. You have to force yourself a lot.

PAM AND ROBERT AYERS

**Pam:** *Your perspective on everything changes. I was diagnosed with breast cancer and it didn't scare me like it might have earlier. I had my surgery and then I was on the plane to the National Rodeo finals. It just never slowed me down.*

**Robert:** *You lose a child, and that's the nth degree. Anything else is no big deal.*

*Robert*: You literally have to work at living.

*Pam*: For a while, every day we woke up thinking, "Is this going to be the day that we're going to find out who did it?" After you're down the road a little ways, you realize that's probably not going to happen. You still hold out hope, but your life begins to take on the resemblance of something normal. You start into a routine, and it does rock along pretty good as a somewhat normal day. But since the arrests last month, that doesn't happen anymore.

*Robert*: The hardest thing now is that we're not in control of our lives at all. We're waiting for the next step, the next phone call, and being told where we need to be. My feeling is if a day goes by and they have something going on and I'm not there, anything could go wrong. So we can't plan anything. We're selling our ranch. I don't enjoy it because I can't be there to take care of my stock and make a living like I did before. We've got to put our lives on hold until this thing is over so we can be at the District Attorney's beck and call, because I'm going to be there.

*Pam*: "Closure." I hate that term with a purple passion. Some say when you finally have a trial and get someone convicted, you reach closure. I don't see closure coming. I mean, you reach another state, but I don't think "closure" is the term because you are never closed with what happened. You live that daily.

*Robert*: I think the reason people use the word "closure" is to give people like us hope and get us through it. But a happy ending is just not going to happen.

*Pam*: We've had some tough times as a couple, but I don't know that there's been a strain on our marriage because we went into it with a good marriage. As a couple, when one's good, the other can be bad. When Robert got a call from the insurance company, he got to where he couldn't talk, but for some reason I was able to, and I didn't cry. So I kind of picked up for him and he's done the same for me.

*Robert*: We had her together and we lost her together.

Our whole theory through this has been to make a positive out of a negative, and that's what kept us going. That's how we came up with our organization S.A.J.E.—Sara, Amy, Jennifer, Elisa.

*Pam:* It's an organization that promotes workplace safety for teenagers. We want other teenagers to be safe in the workplace so other families don't have to go through what we're going through. We also offer support for families. Maybe that's the meaning that our lives are all about now—that we can make a difference in somebody else's life.

*Robert:* If I had my druthers, I would rather have my child murdered than my child be a murderer. I can only imagine what it would be like to raise a child and then to think what he or she had done to another individual. I don't think I could deal with it.

*Pam:* I often think that would be harder to handle. And as bad as our situation is, there are still people worse off. I think of parents who have children missing. So I am thankful for what I have.

— Pam and Robert Ayers

# "Murder is like cancer, the 'C-word.' It's taboo."

There's nothing like murder to make you really, really look at yourself, if you choose. It tears off the scabs from things in the past.

My sister, who was also my best friend, was murdered in June of '94. The man who murdered her lived downstairs. He was running drugs and was worried that she was narcing to the police. Apparently it was the most horrific case the detectives had ever dealt with. You end up feeling like you've won an Oscar for the worst murder of the century.

After her death, I started looking for answers. I reread the Bible but I didn't find the answers I was looking for there. Then I read the *Tibetan Book of Living and Dying,* and that turned me totally around. It talked to me about reincarnation and, that even when there is violence and little dignity in death, there can be dignity restored through helping that person after death. That's a big part of why I do a lot of work with the Center for Victims of Violent Crime. I'm helping my sister in her death and keeping her memory alive. I'm trying to give some honor and dignity back to her. Her spirit is still out there for me.

Murder is like cancer, the "C-word." It's taboo. If you get too close to a family that's had a murder, you're opening yourself to it. And "Murder doesn't happen to people like us, in good neighborhoods"—which is a bunch of crap. Then there's the idea that, "Your sister must have done something to ask for it." So there is quite a bit of shame attached, if you choose to take it on. I put it back where it belongs—to the people who initiated it. I've spent a lot of time recognizing what's mine and what's other people's. I'm not taking somebody else's crap on. I've got enough of my own.

I can't forgive the man who did this. That is the divine's job. It's not my job. If I got the sense that he truly was feeling remorse, was truly rec-

AMY MOKRICKY

*It's like a shattered glass. You can take superglue and glue the pieces back together, but the cracks are always going to be there. It will look whole from a distance, but if you look closely, you're going to see the cracks and seams.*

ognizing what he has done, I think I would want to help him. I want him to see, to live all the repercussions. To walk in each of my family's shoes for a week or so. To know what goes through my brother's mind, my sister's mind. To know that he took my Mom's life as well. To know that he gave my Dad a series of heart attacks. I'd like him to acknowledge that he's destroyed a family because my dad can't deal with any of us. In taking responsibility for having killed somebody, he needs to see his responsibility in having made all these other little deaths.

You trusted life not to injure you this way. You trusted life not to take a beloved person in this way. You trusted humanity not to have that ugly side to it. You trusted your family to be strong, and then instead you had to be strong yourself.

You trust that the judicial system is going to work. You trust that reporters have decency. You have incredible expectations of others' behavior that just doesn't happen. Now I have no trust in others, but I have a greater sense of trust in myself. I know myself a lot better. I see myself as being a lot stronger and more beneficial to the community.

Jill's death has taught me incredible lessons. I have a lot more depth. I consider myself further ahead than people who have not dealt with this type of thing. But my sister's death was a tremendous price to pay for life's lessons.

— Amy Mokricky

*In taking responsibility*
*for having killed somebody,*
*he needs to see his responsibility*
*in having made all these other little deaths.*

# "When the trial was over, we had to deal with each other."

*Herbert*: I look at the crucifixion entirely differently today than I did before. Before, I didn't see the father's love for his son. And I didn't realize how much I loved my boy until he was murdered.

Our son Aytch was bludgeoned to death by his wife's brother Jimmy, who is schizophrenic. Jimmy was off his medication, and Aytch was trying to convince him to go back to the hospital.

I went through anger. I considered revenge. I went through all the natural things that come to people during a tragic event. One by one, I weeded them out and discarded them. You have choices, and we ended up choosing to get involved.

*Emma Jo*: We'd been open with each other all our lives, but then after Aytch's death there was nothing we could talk about. We weren't talking for a couple of years. We could be civil when the children came, but we avoided each other like the plague. He didn't want to hear me, and when he was ready to talk, I didn't want to listen.

*Herbert*: It's like a merry-go-round. One of you is up and the other is down. You just kind of pass each other. You say something, and she comes back kind of sharp. It's not because she's angry, it's because she's hurting. Then, whoa, you start in at each other.

*Emma Jo*: I didn't know a lot of his thoughts until we started presenting together in prison after Aytch's death. When I heard Herbert say he thought of suicide, I just couldn't imagine that from this quiet, loving person. I made a decision. I stood before a group in one of the prisons, telling the story, and I looked at Herbert and said, "You know, I have decided—and you will be the first one to hear it—I will not let

EMMA JO & HERBERT SNYDER

*Emma Jo:* I don't mind "recovery," but don't tell me "closure." That one will get you a black eye!

*Herbert:* It doesn't close. Were we going to stay together? Were we going to get involved or withdraw from society? What did we want to do with this tragedy?

Jimmy have my marriage. He killed my son, and my father died of grief 22 months later. He cannot have my marriage. He cannot!" And our marriage began to mend. It's like new all over again because we were separated, we were going opposite directions.

*Herbert*: When this happened, we were participating in a project that holds seminars for victims and offenders in prison. It works well for both prisoners and victims. I tell the prisoners, "You're my psychiatrist. This is my therapy."

*Emma Jo*: I had a gentleman in the first class who had murdered someone and had served 14 years. One night I looked at him and said, "John, did he beg for you to quit? Did he plead for you to stop beating on him?" He was so shocked that I could look him in the eye and ask him questions like that. It was later I realized these were things I must want to ask Jimmy. John later said in a testimony, "I've spent 14 years satisfied that I murdered that guy. I was cool about it until a lady reached in there and pulled my guts out."

*Herbert*: When Aytch was murdered, I considered revenge. Then I said, "No, God, I won't. You can have Jimmy." I felt a burden lift off my shoulders. It was a reminder that God does exist. He is real. Little by little I evolved. I thought, "If Jesus Christ could forgive me for the things I've done, then why couldn't I forgive Jimmy?" The next time I did a victim impact panel presentation, it just kind of rolled out of my mouth that I'd forgiven Jimmy.

I still wasn't particularly interested in victim-offender mediation though, because it wasn't going to take the hurt away. Then the thought came, "I need to tell Jimmy face to face that I forgive him." And so my outlook toward Jimmy is entirely different. We were talking to a policeman the other day and he called Jimmy names, and I literally flinched inside. And I thought, "Now this is strange!" So I have come full circle.

*Emma Jo*: He forgave Jimmy long before I did. I didn't hate Jimmy, and I thought God would be happy with that. This last year I wrote Jimmy a letter about how I forgave him. It brought a lot of peace. Now we want mediation with Jimmy. Even if it is a one-sided conversation, we need to be able to tell him that we have forgiven him for the murder of our son.

— Emma Jo & Herbert Snyder

*I went through anger.*

*I considered revenge.*

*I went through all the natural things that come to people during a tragic event.*

*One by one, I weeded them out.*

*You have choices,*

*and we ended up choosing to get involved.*

# "I needed to find my way."

My son was an artist and had a degree in visual communications. He was very much a homebody. He never missed coming home for dinner on Sundays; we had a very close relationship. He was planning to go back to school and was driving a cab as a kind of stop-off. At 4:00 on an afternoon in October, 1994, he picked up two young men, 14 and 17 years old, at the train station. When they got in the car, they said, "This is a stickup." He got out of the car and turned his back, and they shot him.

In the beginning, I didn't want to live, but then I got to the place where I felt, "I have to go on with my life. I have my other children, and I have to help them get through this, too." My grandson was killed three months before, shot in the head in a drive-by shooting! He was killed in July, and I was trying to help my other son through this. He was a single parent because my grandson's mother had passed away. Then my son was killed in October. The very same chaplain that met me at the hospital when my grandson was shot was the chaplain that met me when my son was shot. She could never get over that and neither could I.

I remember thinking right away, "I don't know why this happened, but it's happening, and I've got to find a way to live with it." I understood that no matter what happens, God was there with me. I really did some earnest praying, asking God to help me. If I wouldn't have been strong in my faith, I probably could have lost my mind.

Sometimes it was kind of scaring me that I wasn't angry. I was angry to an extent, but I never felt rage. I feel strongly that if I take on anger, it will overpower my ability to go on and to put my pieces together for me and my family. That's more important than being angry.

You have to choose what you're going to allow to bother you, because otherwise you can't

LOUISE WILLIAMS

*It was just like dropping a glass and everything shattered, then trying to pick up one or two pieces at a time to put them back together. My faith was the main thing that got me through, that and my family—my other children and my grandchildren. But most of all, I knew that my son would want me to go on.*

43

get from point A to point B. So I concentrated on surviving and helping my family through, and these experiences pulled my family very close. We always had family time, but now we have family time together every Sunday. We all try to keep in very close contact.

I'm a district justice and had just been sworn in for another term. I made the decision that I was going to complete my term because that's what I needed and what my son would have wanted me to do. I did take a leave of absence for about six months. My counselor said, "Life is like riding a train. Every now and then it's okay to get off and plot your way." That's the way I was feeling. I just needed to get off for awhile and find my way.

The offender who shot my son got a life sentence. I felt the system worked and justice was given, but there's still loss on each side. It's unfortunate because two lives were taken—the life of the 14-year-old who shot my son, and my son's life.

I haven't really put into words that I have forgiven them, but it is in my mind that I need to work on that. I can't say it's a heavy burden, but I think when I can say freely that I've forgiven them, then I'm there. I don't know whether to use the word "healing," but maybe it is the proper word in that respect, when I can actually say I forgave them for what they did. I've never really said that.

To some extent I feel sorry for them. It must be a horrible thing for the 14-year-old, to be in prison for the rest of his life. But I feel more anger toward his mother than toward him. Somebody that's 14 years old and had no remorse whatsoever must not have had any love at all. At least I can say, "I have some very good memories of my son." He never harmed anybody that I know of; he was a good person. And I know that he knew what love was because I truly loved him and he truly loved me; we both knew that. My son knew the love of a family.

I'll never forget a friend of mine who's a priest. He came when my son was killed and we talked. I told him my parents died 37 days apart, very suddenly, at the same age I am now. He said, "Louise, this is your psalm: You are a survivor and because you are, you're going to get through this." I think about that a lot.

I think I'm healing, that I'm just about there. I don't think I'll ever be healed to the point that it's not part of my life every day, but I can function.

I view life as taking a trip on a train. You have to get off sometimes and look around. Then you get back on and keep traveling. You have to go on. You can't stop the journey until it's time for the journey to stop.

— Louise Williams

*The offender who shot my son got a life sentence.*

*But I feel more anger toward his mother than toward him.*

*Somebody that's 14 years old*

*and had no remorse whatsoever*

*must not have had any love at all.*

*"It's like destroying the old structure and rebuilding."*

# "I needed to decide whether to live or not."

My older sister's marriage broke up. Her husband was in a lot of emotional turmoil and ended up taking it out on my younger sister Pat. He strangled Pat, then slit her throat. I was the one who found her. This happened in 1980.

I experienced anguish, a visceral, animal anguish. I felt like a mother bear that has lost her cub and stands in the forest roaring, "Uhhh!" My anger and frustration didn't end with the murder in 1980—it started all over and even intensified 10 years later when this man was up for parole

A few years after my sister's murder I joined the police force. I know now that doing that was part of my escape. I took on a mission to try to block my pain. I needed to help other people, to feel like I was doing something. I didn't look at my feelings until 13 years later. It took me that long to realize that I was in trouble emotionally.

In 1991 I found out that this man had been released on parole and I had not been notified. He was in a half-way house in the area that I policed! That upset me. What would have happened if I had seen him or had to pick him up? What would I have done? I carry a gun! My fear of my level of rage was a trigger for me to do something about myself.

I had watched other police officers deal with the constant in-your-face violence, and had seen them lose it and beat on offenders. I remember one specific incident of having to pull another officer off a suspect. I felt his level of rage building, and I realized that because I hadn't dealt with my sister's death, I was in jeopardy of becoming like those other officers who lost it. I was in trouble, and I needed help.

I had avoided therapy for 13 years. But I realized now that I needed to decide whether to live or not. It was pretty much a matter of life and death. That was a crucial turning point.

**KIM MUZYKA**

*For years I lived with a brick of death inside my chest. It wasn't until the thirteenth year that I started on that brick with a chisel. Sometimes a big piece comes off. Sometimes it's just little fragments—but it gets smaller and smaller. It's not gone—maybe it will never go – but I visualize it now as a small rock. It's not a concrete block anymore.*

I wasn't just dealing with my sister's death. It took three years of therapy to identify my other personal traumas. I call them "trauma bubbles," because they're all self-contained, and yet they connect. You don't just deal with them one at a time; I think of it more like peeling onion layers.

It's like destroying an old structure and rebuilding. There are times when I've felt I wasn't going to survive the process, but then I would start to visualize the building of a new structure. I saw mine as a huge cliff. It's like in "Sleeping Beauty," that huge cliff where they have a battle. It's dark and jagged, and you have to fall off it before you can move to the other side of this beautiful mountain. It's still a climb to get there, but it's like visualizing a feeling of health and strength.

Thirteen years after the murder I got involved with the victim offender mediation program. My first meeting with the offender was satisfying simply because I was validated in my opinion of the man. He denied responsibility, blamed the system for his problems, defended himself. I just got angry, but that's stronger than feeling vulnerable. I thought, "Okay, he's in jail and that's where he needs to be." The second meeting, at his request, was terrible. He hadn't changed. He had no remorse, no recognition of the trauma he had caused others, including his children. I remember feeling, "I don't need to participate in his rehabilitation. I don't need to take on his stuff."

I've made another choice. I don't want just to function; I want to heal. I want to transcend this, and I feel that I'm 70-80% there. I am actually starting to be able to visualize excitement for living! That enthusiasm is not always there, but I visualize crossing the border from victim to survivor. I'm still a work in progress!

— Kim Muzyka

I realized
that because I hadn't dealt with my sister's death,
I was in jeopardy of becoming like those other officers
who lost it.
I was in trouble,
and I needed help.

# "People want to define me by my adversity and grief."

The ironic thing is that, for Kathy's sake, she would have been better to die in the building. Thirty-five of her closest workers, including her very best friend Susan, were killed in the Oklahoma City bombing. She attended those funerals, buried most of those 35 people, and it was very draining for her. Kathy had been fighting clinical depression before the bombing, and she had a fair amount of survival guilt. She felt like she should have died instead of Susan, who was young and full of life. For the next three years it was tough to watch her continue to sink deeper and deeper into depression. On March 9, 1998, she swallowed large quantities of medicine, and she died on March 18. So she's another victim of the bombing—it really finished her off.

Kathy founded the Metropolitan Fair Housing Council in 1978, and the city has really opened up in large measure due to her work in civil rights. Since her death she's been accepted into the Women's Hall of Fame, and the Oklahoma Human Rights Commission gave her an award for her work in civil rights. My way of handling the grief is to find all the areas of Kathy's life that I can continue. I'm honored that I've been selected to be on the Board of Trustees for the Fair Housing Council. I've taken over the editing of the neighborhood newsletter, something she had done for 25 years. I feel connected to her when I do the newsletter. And I'm very active in the church that both of us belonged to. I feel like I'm carrying on the kind of work she would have done if she were still alive.

Those involvements in the community keep me going. I've been blessed by a tremendous support system because the church and neighborhood rallied around me. I can't picture pulling up roots from this home and neighborhood.

It's both a source of joy and pain for me to drive around the city and see these things—the

FRANK SILOVSKY

*Mourning and celebration are really intertwined, I think. I feel the loss of Kathy, but I also look at mourning as a tribute to the person. Without mourning, you could just dispense with the image and memory of the person. There would be no tribute—and I want to pay tribute to her. I'm proud to have been her husband.*

Housing Council Office, the Memorial site, our neighborhood garden. We have a vegetable garden that the neighborhood works on together. Nearby there's a flower garden in memory of Kathy. Every time I see it, I'm reminded of her.

The Memorial Foundation made seedlings from the survivor elm available to survivors and families. I got a seedling and planted it in our front yard, and I used part of Kathy's ashes to plant the tree. We also planted a Bradford pear, one of Kathy's favorite trees, in a city park near a tree planted for her friend Susan, and we scattered ashes at the base. The Bradford pear tree blooms right around the time of the year that Kathy died.

About 75 people came to plant the tree in the park. We had a very good ceremony. Then we all went to the church and had a dinner together. Many people spoke about Kathy, telling their connections to her. All of that's been therapy for me.

I think I'm pretty damn resilient. My daughter knows that and doesn't worry about me much. My son worries because he thinks I cry too much. But tears are my way of venting; I feel a release when I cry. I probably cry more than the average male, but that doesn't bother me. I do think my better friends are female because women are so much better at dealing with feelings. The men I know who have suffered the loss of loved ones tend to stuff it. They think it's a sign of weakness to cry or even show sadness.

I've had to resist people defining me by my grief or my adversity. Not only did Kathy die, but I had a bad bicycle accident. Then Peggy, a woman with whom I had established an important relationship, died of a brain aneurysm. When I came to church after this, a member said, "My God, what's next?" I have to resist that; I don't like being the person who's had two women die and a bad accident. I'm much more than that! And I don't believe I'm star-crossed. I really think I'm gifted by being surrounded by good things and people.

I am angry at Tim McVeigh because he made the last three years of Kathy's life so miserable. She could have survived without his act. I think it would be more painful if the perpetrators were not brought to justice, so it gives me some peace of mind to know that those two men are not going to be able to repeat what they did. But I am against the death penalty, and I do not approve of killing Tim McVeigh. Transcending to me means moving on. Kathy would want me to. I know that, and I'm doing that.

— Frank Silovsky

*I feel like*
*I'm carrying on the kind of work*
*she would have done*
*if she were still alive.*

# "You don't know how you're going to respond until you're in it."

You don't know how strong your faith is until it's really tested. And you don't know how tough a person you are, or how you're going to respond, until you're in it. This put my faith through the wringer, but it was strong enough to come out.

My husband was a campus minister. He was coming home around 10:15 Tuesday night, January 28, 1997. I heard a loud noise and looked out the window, and I saw someone lying in the street with blood coming out of his head. Then I saw my husband's car and realized it was him. The police are working hard, but they still have almost nothing on the case.

I had thought it was pretty good to go through childbirth without anesthesia. I thought, "Whooo, I'm tough." Compared to this, that was nothing!

I was in a kind of shock for four months. Sometimes I feel like all I did for a couple of years was grieve. Right away, though, I got into counseling, and I got the kids into a group session for grieving kids. I read books on grieving. The church has been helpful, and I joined a widow's group for people with Christian faith. I know more widows than I wish I ever knew!

People say, "How do you explain that he died?" I've thought about it a million times, and I can't explain it. But I'm not going to dwell on that forever. Good and bad people die, and a good person died that night. The Bible never says that if you are a good person, you're going to have long years, or that if I am doing good works, I'm going to be favored. There's no absolute guarantee. I never thought there was; my husband never thought there was. I believe I had a good theology going into this—otherwise, my faith would have been shattered.

I've been angry at God sometimes. At times I think, "This isn't fair; it really sucks!" There are still times when I wonder, "Can I trust God?"

**SHERRI BRUNSVOLD**

*I've rebuilt my life—a new life—and it works. This is the life I have; I go on from here. I'd say it's a good life. I'd give anything to go back, but I can live with the fact that I can't go back. I feel like I've handled it overall pretty well, considering. I guess I'm strong, but I get tired of people saying that.*

57

But I think that's okay with God. In fact, I would say I'm closer to God because we've had some pretty good dialogues—I throw it at him! You should be able to do that if you have a close relationship.

I think what helped was I was able to talk about it a lot, and I didn't mind crying. I never felt like I had to be strong for the kids—I let them see that it's okay to cry. What happened was a bad thing, and it's okay to cry about bad things.

Someone told my eight-year-old son Justin, "Now you're the man of the family." I told him, "Justin, you're a boy. You don't need to take care of me. I have friends helping me do that. You don't need to turn into a man." I don't want my children to feel like thy have to take care of me.

Before my husband and I moved here, we worked with an inner city ministry in Chicago. We didn't want a cushy life; we wanted to make a difference in the world. We never thought, "We're going to get killed," but we never knew what tomorrow was going to bring. Maybe that helped me to prepare for this. And maybe it helped that I grew up on a farm. Farmers can't control the weather or the grain prices. My parents didn't bring me up with the idea that if you work really hard, you'll be successful. They just took life one day at a time.

I think it would be real emotional for me if they caught somebody for this. Maybe some of the anger I've felt at God I'd feel toward them. I wonder why they did it. So I want them to be caught. But I don't want to go through all the stuff that would be involved.

I kind of like it that sometimes people don't know what I've gone through. I don't want everybody to know my life story, and I don't need to know theirs. I don't want everybody to feel sorry for me, and I don't want people to know me as, "That's the widow of the minister that was shot." I want them to know me as, "Oh, that's Sherri."

Women will be complaining about their husbands and sometimes I feel like snapping at them. I miss what I had. But then, for the most part, I don't want their lives. This is the life I have, and I go on from here. I feel like I've accomplished a lot, that I'm strong. The situation is sad, but how I've responded isn't.

Before this I had an easy life; then all of a sudden it went the opposite way. I've learned that all that matters is how you respond to what happens. You use everything you have—your faith, your friends, your personality. And you have choices. I lost some of those choices, but I still had to make choices with what was left. That's the meaning of life!

*Update January 7, 2001:* In April, 2000, an arrest was made in my husband's case. A young man (with a pretty big record), who lived down the street from us, was arrested. He was 16 back in January of 1997! He told a few social workers in a juvenile detention facility where he lived that he was involved, that he himself shot the minister.

The trial was in September, and on October 2nd he was convicted of second degree murder. In Pennsylvania that is life without chance of parole.

He never admitted to the crime after the arrest and took the stand himself, denying he said those things to the social workers. He showed no emotion during the whole trial or the reading of the verdict.

I brought my kids to the sentencing so they could hear me read my victim's impact statement and see this man who killed their dad. I don't think we have any hatred towards him. It is good to know who did it and that he is off the streets. What a waste of his own life, too!

So it was quite a year. We are doing well for the most part. God has blessed us with great friends and given us lots of strength!

— Sherri Brunsvold

# "I was stuck on April 19, 1995."

I was just like any other slug out there working for a living. I'd get into some arguments about political issues like the death penalty, but I wasn't involved. Then my 23-year-old daughter Julie was killed in the 1995 bombing of the Alfred P. Murrah Federal Building in Oklahoma City.

At first I was in absolute pain. All I wanted was to see those two people fried. I was smoking three packs of cigarettes a day and drinking heavily. I was physically and mentally sick. I was stuck on April 19, 1995. Looking back, I call that the temporary insanity period.

I went down to the bomb site and stood right underneath the survivor tree. A statement that Julie made got to echoing in my mind. We were driving across Iowa and heard a radio story about an execution in Texas. Julie's reaction was, "Dad, all they are doing is teaching hate to their children." I didn't think a hell of a lot about it at the time, but then, after she was dead, I got to thinking about it.

I knew that the death penalty wasn't going to bring her back, and I realized that it was about revenge and hate. And the reason Julie and 167 others were dead was because of the very same thing: revenge and hate. It was McVeigh and Nichols' hate against the federal government. They would never have performed that act if they hadn't felt justified that they were doing the right thing for their cause, just like we think we're doing the right thing for our cause when we execute prisoners.

In April 1996 a reporter said to me, "Bud, I bet you'll be happy when McVeigh and Nichols are tried and executed." I just shook my head and said, "No, that's not what I want." The look from her eyes was, "Here I just spent 45 minutes talking to this man about his wonderful daughter, and he's insane."

BUD WELCH

*I don't know what it is to be a born-again Christian—I'm a Roman Catholic and we don't talk about that much—but maybe this is what it means: to be able to pull through the absolute terror.*

I went on to explain the journey I had been on, and it started to make sense to her. She said, "Bud, can I use this?"

When you're raised on a dairy farm in central Oklahoma and run a service station for 35 years, you're not very media-wise. I said, "Hell, why not?"

For the next weeks my telephone rang off the hook—not just the media, but private citizens, too. I finally discovered that what they really were calling about was to find out who this nut was that they had uncovered under a rock in Oklahoma. But I'd tell them, step by step, of the journey I was on.

Once I turned loose of that revenge and hate, the feel-good was tremendous. After that, I was able to get things sorted out. I started getting a handle on my drinking and cutting back on smoking. I was able to start reconciling things within myself. It's a process, though. I still have moments of rage that hit me, but they're spaced out more than they used to be.

People ask, "Did you pray a lot to arrive at that?" I don't know how many damn Hail Mary's I said, but I wasn't praying. I was just saying words. I said that recently in a talk, and a bishop spoke up and said, "Whether you know it or not, God heard some of those prayers." So yeah, some of them got there.

Now I'm an active opponent of the death penalty. People ask, "Are you doing this because of Julie?" That's probably part of it. I'm carrying her flag, and I have a feeling that I want the whole world to know who my kid was. When people ask me to come to speak, then I have thousands more ears that I can tell who my kid was!

— Bud Welch

*I knew that the death penalty wasn't going to bring her back,*
*and I realized that it was about*
*revenge and hate.*
*And the reason Julie and 167 others were dead*
*was because of the very same thing:*
*revenge and hate.*

# "I fell into this deep, dark hole with no steps."

In 1992 I was kidnapped by a man I didn't know, raped, beaten badly, and left to die in a remote wilderness area. Fortunately, I was rescued by five teenagers camping nearby.

When I woke up I knew I was in serious danger, that the injuries were life-threatening. I don't remember a lot, but I remember hearing birds starting to chirp. They were like messengers; they were saying I was still alive. I still appreciate life when I wake up every day. I'm very grateful to be able to walk and talk. Some people who have sustained injuries such as mine spend years trying to learn that.

The deposition taken during the court proceedings was the most horrible experience I ever had—Wolkstein and Kramer's *Inanna: Queen of Heaven and Earth*, in which the queen of heaven has to go through seven gates and remove a piece of her clothing each time. By the time she reaches her enemy she is naked. That's exactly how I felt by the time I was done, stripped of everything including my dignity.

Then, at another hearing, the offender escaped! He ran down the road, and a friend, my husband's business partner, caught him. What if my friend hadn't been there? Would he have gotten caught? I was terrified.

There was a time when I was very angry. How could a God let this happen to me? Why am I here? I don't think I've gotten the "why" answered, but I don't think it's as important as it was. I can't find an answer to "Why me?", and that seems to take a lot of energy.

I was adopted and don't know my heritage, but I've felt attuned to Native American culture, especially after studying about healing in indigenous cultures in school. I use some of their rituals. I made a peace pipe with beads that tell a story. That was healing for me. I also built a sweat lodge and my husband and I use it. Those rituals seem important to me, and I

SUSAN RUSSELL

*Most of the time I feel like a survivor, though sometimes I feel like a victim. Like two years ago,*
*I found in the public records pictures of me that weren't supposed to be there. I felt like a victim,*
*but what I did about it was the survivor in me. We all choose the paths we take in the aftermath.*
*We can choose to be victims, or we can choose to be survivors.*

believe they have become important to my husband as well. So we do these little rituals together, and I think it's important. It is part of the healing path.

When I spoke in a class recently, there was a Mexican-Indian women who was a survivor. After I talked, she brought me some sage and flowers and hugged me. She put her hand here on my heart. I just cried and cried. I guess you would call that a ritual, too. It was wonderful; it's what I needed. I'll never forget that experience.

At the time of the trial I just wanted my offender to die. I've tried so hard, but I don't know how much that's changed. Sometimes I just feel like I'm walking a line, a really fine line, between forgiveness and hatred. I just don't know what forgiveness is supposed to be. Different people interpret it differently. I interpret it that I don't think about him every second of every day. Then when I listen to people in church, I feel like everything is a jumble. I don't know where I am with this.

It was very important to me that the offender be punished. He took so much from me, and I've felt like he needed to have things taken from him. I've wanted him to feel the intense pain that I felt. I've also felt that he had to pay. The cost of all this was astronomical. I asked for restitution but was denied because he doesn't have any money. I wanted to put that money away in a fund to provide scholarships for victims who want to go back to school, because going back to school was very important for me. The fact that he got away without having to pay anything makes me really angry. He's not even taking responsibility or recognizing that he did this.

I've changed dramatically, but I like myself and the things I'm doing. I like learning that I can set boundaries. I like the fact that I'm not nice and sweet. And I don't think I'd be writing or focusing on a career in criminal justice policy otherwise. I'd still be guiding people through the woods and working as a ski patroller. I don't think I knew myself the way I know myself now. I was too busy trying to be a good skier.

My whole world is different now. I grieve who I used to be. She is gone, buried. She was innocent, very social, very outgoing, very carefree. Now when I'm in a place where I feel safe for a minute or an hour, I treasure that. I need to spend time alone now to think and reflect and write. Writing has been a really good outlet for me. Relationships have changed too. I have just a small circle of close friends now.

I fight with shame and humiliation all the time. But I think I recognized my courage when I wrote my culminating thesis, "Myths, Heroes, Heroines and the Heroic Journey." After researching the journey of a hero or heroine in myths from several cultures, I realized that I had indeed taken the path of a heroine/survivor. Writing this fulfilled a goal I had, which was to go public with my story. I felt I was not only helping others, but beginning to heal some of my scars left by the experience.

When I got depressed during the first three to four years, I felt like I fell into this deep, dark hole with no steps. When my husband or a friend did something for me, they were handing down a rope. Now when I face a hole, I have the tools I need to find somebody to help pull me out. And it's my time to hand down the rope to others, recognizing that I still might need the rope myself sometimes. In my work as a victim advocate, I'm giving something back.

*Update, a year later:* Last year I really thought the old Sue was gone and never coming back. I missed her. In the past year, I feel she's come back in various ways; for instance, being a little bit more social. I see bits and pieces of her where I never used to. I've been cherishing that.

I do want or need to spend a lot of time by myself now. Recently I went hiking by myself with my dog, something I hadn't done in eight years. That was partly the old Sue, but also the new Sue taking on the fears and wanting that time alone to reflect on things.

I wish it had never happened, but I keep thinking about all the positive things that have come out of this. I just received my master's degree; I'm working as Coordinator for Victim Services 2000. And my husband and I have grown closer than we used to be. It's a new field, new growth, and I really like that.

— Susan Russell

# "The jury found him not guilty. I was devastated."

On the night of the shooting, they wheeled me into my room before surgery. My new roommate is looking at the TV and they show my house. The guy says, "Man, they shot and killed this man and woman!" I said, "No, they didn't kill me." He said, "Oh, man—that was your wife? I'm so sorry. Man, you know what? You got a nice house." I could not help but laugh. I had just gone through the most traumatic thing in my life, and all this guy has to say is that I have a nice house. But I had to get back on my feet and get this nice house back in order!

After our 1986 wedding, a former boyfriend of Sharon's started following her. Her car was vandalized a number of times. Then, in 1992, the stalker's brother came to the door and said he had a gift for her. He had a shotgun. I grabbed my girls and ran to the back bedroom; then I charged him. He shot me, and then went after Sharon. They were loading me in the ambulance when I heard it come over the radio, "Second victim, DOA." I said, "They're talking about my wife!" The attendant just nodded. At that moment, the first thought that came to my mind was, "I'm going to raise my girls."

My girls were 4 years and 5 months old. Sharon and I had shared responsibilities for taking care of them, but in the house, Sharon was necessity and I was entertainment. So I had to start taking care of my family. I wasn't prepared for it to be this way, but it wasn't going to be an impossible task.

When I was a young man, my grandmother, who had raised me, suffered a stroke. From 1978 to 1990, when she passed, I was pretty much her primary caretaker. After a full day's work, I would drive across town to the house I grew up in, and I would feed her, bathe her, put her to bed. I guess that gave me strength to be able to take care of someone who needs it.

RICARDO WIGGS

*People say, "You're really a strong guy." I go, "I'm no stronger than you are." It's a decision. Strength is measured by what you decide to do.*

There was a trial and the jury found him not guilty. I was devastated. It was as if 12 people stood there and reloaded the shotgun. When I walked out of the courtroom, I told a television reporter, "When I left my house this morning, I told my daughter that Daddy would get the bad man that killed Mommy. Now I have to go home and tell them I didn't."

A major decision for me was not to take revenge. I'd never been a man of evil spirit. I don't walk about with a Bible. But I always knew it was my place in this life to do the right thing, and vindication would not have been the right thing. But I do still have to continually fight those thoughts. They come to mind at times like anniversaries or holidays.

Another decision I made was to move forward. I felt if I didn't make progress in my professional life as a systems analyst, I would have failed in supporting my family. But the decision to help others was not one that was hard because this has been a part of my life. My grandmother was a person who helped everyone, and, when no one was there to help her, I knew it was my job.

I lost my grandmother, I lost Sharon; then I lost my mother. Three key women in my life who made a difference in me being who I am, in how I lived my life—all left me in the '90s. Having these things happen made me not strong, but accepting. There is delivery, and acceptance is the biggest part of delivery—acceptance that this will be my life, that this is normal. This is where I am now. I'm going to change what I can and accept what I cannot change.

I will never have full justice in my case. Full justice would have been a conviction. But making sure that some other people are going to be safe is justice for me. I worked to enforce stiffer penalties for stalking, because that was the cause of my wife's death. Maryland did pass the bill, and now there's an interstate stalking bill that was signed by the President. I was invited to the White House to witness the signing. So there is justice.

I want to be known as a survivor rather than a victim. I've been through the loss of my grandmother, the family's neglect of her caretaking in her final years. I've survived my mother's cancer. I've been through homicide and have been shot myself—I've been that close to death. I'm like the paperboy: no matter what happens—rain, snow—you're going to see me deliver the news.

— Ricardo Wiggs

*We went through the trial, and I hit bottom.*

*Then I realized that this is my life,*

*this is what I have to live with.*

*Everything I had worked for,*

*everything that was me before this,*

*was not gone,*

*but I had misplaced it.*

*"The light of hope for me
is that justice will eventually be done."*

# "He has become an obsession with me."

After Joey's murder, I would go to the cemetery and sit a lot. Once I sat through a thunder and lightning storm, a really bad storm. It was raining so hard and lightning was shooting all over. I was yelling at God and nature, "You're angry. Well, I'm angrier than you are. I can outscream you!" Lightning was striking all around and I just yelled louder, "Why did this happen? I want him back." I would scream "Joey" at the top of my lungs. It was a battle between me and nature. Eventually the storm stopped, and there was a rainbow. I was soaking wet and I couldn't talk for two days, but it was worth it.

I'm Joe Brucker's mother. I didn't have a very good marriage and Joe became my support.

He was my son, my friend, my brother. He was just my heart and soul. Then he was murdered in 1998 at 17 years old, gunned down in my car. The killer fired at him eight times.

This young man Korey was tried in 1999 and found not guilty. When he was taken out of the courtroom, he turned and winked at me, so he made it personal. Because of this threat, where I can go is limited; it's like I became the one in prison.

Korey has become an obsession with me—I promised that I would make him pay for murdering my son, and most of my energy goes into that. At the beginning, I wanted to kill him. Then I realized that I would go to jail and that would leave my other son without a parent. So I just started keeping the offender's case alive and active in the system so he doesn't become a lost file. The light of hope for me is that justice will eventually be done. Then I'll have peace and Joey will have peace. I have a baby lying in the ground and nobody's being held accountable for hurting him.

My heart was broken, and there was nothing here enough to make me want to continue going

DEBORAH BRUCKER

*Someone—I think it was Emerson—said that clouds are rafts for the soul. I watch the clouds take different shapes and wonder which one Joey is on.*

on. Then my younger son Matthew came to me one day, grabbed my hands, and says, "Look at me. I'm still here. You still have dreams—you have *my* dreams. Don't die with Joey. Don't let Korey take both of you away from me." And at that moment I was looking into his brother's eyes. It seemed like Matthew became two in one.

I've found a good man who understands how I feel. We're getting married and we're going to have a little table to the right of the altar with Joey's picture and a candle. Everyone will be carrying a solitary rose because that's my symbol with Joey. I'm not throwing the rose. My rose is gonna go on his grave.

— Deborah Brucker

**Update**: *During the day that this interview was taking place, on the afternoon before Deborah's wedding, the young man accused of murdering her son was arrested on another charge. This one was expected to stick.*

Lightning was striking all around and I just yelled louder,
"Why did this happen? I want him back."
Eventually the storm stopped,
and there was a rainbow.
I was soaking wet and I couldn't talk for two days,
but it was worth it.

# "Justice is knowing and acting on the truth, and I don't know the whole truth."

After my sister's murder, I felt morally obligated to take the life of her killer. I discovered the training I had received in the armed forces had not been dispelled. I'm right there on the edge; I should think almost any ex-solder is right on the edge. It's scary because you realize you're not that different from the murderer.

Mary was a promising young educator. She was murdered in 1978, soon after she turned 34. I realized how close we were after she was gone; I've never found that kind of a friend since. I think about her every day. When I'm alone and forget myself for an instant, I find myself saying, "Good-bye, Mary" or "Mary, help me." It just wells up and bursts from my repressed consciousness.

There never was a trial. Within two days the police narrowed the range of suspects to just her husband. He had purchased a revolver about six months before she was killed and had taken out four insurance policies on her life. But the district attorney was reluctant to bring the case to trial because he feared it would be lost.

Mary's husband collected the insurance money, kept the educational center that my sister and he had established, and still collects the royalties on her books. To our family, it appeared that here was a man who deliberately, for his own profit, destroyed a life, then proceeded to defy the family, the laws of California, and the moral law, and to profit from this crime. It appeared to be the perfect crime.

The law failed us, and we've had to respond outside the structure of the law. We made every effort to reconstruct the events preceding the crime. We've got it all together, but probably it's not proof beyond reasonable doubt in a court of law. We have also been tortured with the thought that we might be mistaken. It's happened before that innocent people have been convicted and put to death. Fairness required us

**JOSEPH PRESTON BARATTA**

*I discovered I had revengeful impulses in me. I also discovered that I had very generous qualities reflected in my decision to be of service to humanity by studying the history of efforts to strengthen the rule of law through the United Nations. My scholarly work is motivated by the murder of my sister; it is a creative response to a violent injury.*

to inquire whether there could be other explanations for what happened. But all other possibilities have disappeared.

For the first few years, I went through the most primitive of all tortures. I felt morally responsible to put the murderer of my sister to death. I felt it was my moral duty—if the police failed, the family must intervene. It was a scene right out of a primitive blood feud. No one said openly that's what I ought to do, but there were looks and remarks from people that indicated they expected that.

I didn't know what to do. I'd done a tour in the Marine Corps and I know how to handle weapons. But I didn't want to kill. I thought to myself, "I could be wrong. I could fail. I could injure someone else." And I thought, "This would just be adding another wrong to the wrongs we've suffered."

It was like the Vietnam war all over again: Do we return evil for evil or good for evil? My father said that if we were Christians, we could not do to the offender what he did to us. My mother said we must act in a dignified way. I said we must seek justice. But I chose not to act in the spirit of the blood feud. So we looked for alternative responses.

My folks went to an early grave, brokenhearted. So now I'm the sole survivor, and I am pursuing justice as I understand it. I've been trying various devices to affect the prime suspect's conscience in the spirit of Matthew 5, the Sermon on the Mount. I've tried to meet with him, but he has refused. I've also engaged a researcher to prepare a professional evaluation of Mary's con-

tributions to education. She was a phenomenon during her life, and I want to preserve her work. It's a way of trying to correct the destruction of her life. I'm showing that I'm not powerless, even 21 years later. I have not laid down and died. I am struggling to preserve her life and memory.

Elizabeth Kübler-Ross describes four stages of grief on the death of a loved one. First is disbelief, then comes anger, then comes depression. Last comes acceptance. I've never reached the stage of acceptance. I feel I'm obliged to change reality—the reality that somebody saw it to his private advantage to kill my sister and imagines that he can do so with impunity, in defiance of the laws of the state and of moral laws.

My objective is to expose him or bring him to justice or, best of all, awaken his conscience so that he should seek some kind of forgiveness. In the spirit of the Sermon on the Mount, I can tell you I'm prepared to forgive. But I'm unwilling to forgive without signs of repentance.

Quite early I reached the point where I refused to lay this crime at the foot of God. I don't think God had anything to do with it. This is a crime committed by a man. The whole idea of a just God with an inscrutable purpose has disappeared from my thinking. I don't think God did this to punish me, nor do I think there is some greater purpose being served by it. I regard the whole matter as a failure of humanity.

I have decided that I cannot believe in the good governance of a caring God. I continue to go to our Quaker meeting, and I understand God as an imminent God, a spirit we can hear in our hearts. It's a still, small voice. But there's not a transcendent God who created the world and governs it.

I tried to understand those public issues that involve the taking of life, particularly abortion, defensive war, and capital punishment. I've come to the view that with respect to premeditated murder, the death penalty *would* help to restore the standard of wrong in our country and deter such crimes.

Justice is knowing and acting on the truth, and I don't know the truth, the whole truth. I preferred that this case come to a court of law where the evidence could be presented fairly to the community and everyone could judge, based on due process of law and standards of evidence. The punishment for the person who murdered my sister ought to be settled by the community through its laws. I want to affirm the rule of law in this case of mine. If this man were convicted, I would be satisfied with whatever punishment the judge would award—20 years, life imprisonment, death. I would like to know the truth; I'm willing to let others determine the punishment.

As a family we have searched for our God in this case. We've searched for the nature of justice. We've searched for a way to find forgiveness and reconciliation. But there's one more thing, and it's important, too. I became dedicated to some positive work in my life, and this was to finish my Ph.D. studies in international diplomatic history. I wrote a dissertation on efforts to strengthen the United Nations. Following my Marine Corps service, I've been devoted to the peace movement. I try to serve the cause of peace by disentangling intellectually the practical efforts to strengthen the rule of law through our international institutions.

It's a big, complex problem, but it's at the heart of our future as human beings. I've published two books and several monographs and articles and made myself into a kind of internationally known historian of the very narrow field of United Nations reform and the cause of world federal government.

The injustice done to my family was small compared, say, to the injustice of the Jews killed in the Holocaust or all the people connected to the 60 million who were killed in World War II. But I have been sensitized to the issue of justice, and I'm doing what I can in that field. That's my response to the murder of my sister, although I don't dramatize this by telling people what happened to me. Nobody in the department of history at my college knows this.

For me, the principle virtue in life is courage. I live life like a soldier in battle. I have to charge up the hill against darkness, human viciousness, ignorance. I'm a soldier for peace.

I must say, after 21 years I seem to be able to handle this. But until a year or two ago, I couldn't talk about it without crying. I think it was because I kept it bottled up so much. Then I began to risk telling this story. I'm aware that I could lose friends by sharing this, and I don't tell people until I'm really pressed. It's been a mercy and a help to be able to talk about this after all these years.

— Joseph Preston Baratta

# "Was it something I did that contributed to her death?"

In my experience, the key to how people respond when they become victims is where they were prior to their victimization. What was going on in their lives, what were their personality traits, what capabilities and professional experiences either prepared them or further exacerbated their victimization? The decisions people make are based on these prior experiences and expertise.

My mother was raped and murdered in her home in 1990. The investigation was mishandled, and the primary suspect became my father. My father had been a stroke victim 28 months before the murder and couldn't walk or stand without a walker!

When we tried to help defend him, we became part of the investigation. When I asked to be my father's official representative, they threatened me with obstruction of justice. So we hired a defense attorney and they started telling

everyone, "The Torres family has hired a defense attorney so they have something to hide." None of our legitimate questions and pleas for assistance were taken as anything other than diverting the investigators from what they thought was the right suspect.

That began my education about the justice system. I felt I needed to gather as much information as I possibly could, because until we did, there was no way we could prove these people wrong. My background as a researcher helped. I established a pattern that we were being lied to by officials, that there was significant incompetence, that the right hand didn't know what the left hand was doing.

After the murder, things got real bad at the house. I'd come home and I'd cry. I cried at work. I yelled at my wife. The littlest thing would set me off. I was so angry all the time.

We made an appointment with the priest to help us through our emotional problems. He lis-

**VINCENT TORRES**

*Getting my father vindicated was a transforming moment. It was like, "You sons-of-bitches, I told you he wasn't the person and you wouldn't believe me. Now I have proof."*

tened, and after awhile he looked at his watch and said, "Well, I need to go play golf this afternoon so I'd like us to say a prayer." The next communication we got from the church was, "It's time for tithing—please sign up." The church has programs for people who are divorced, but no programs for people who suffer victimization. So the experience made me question the whole system we have in life here, from the criminal justice system to the church.

I had expected my mom to teach my kids cultural issues. I don't know how to make tamales! Now who is going to teach them to make tamales? Our tradition was to have Mom come spend Christmas with us, and for the first two years we didn't celebrate Christmas, period. We didn't know how to fill that vacancy at the table. It was too painful to think about the memories.

My wife said at some point, "Nicole's going to be three years old. You need to put up a tree for her. Your mother would have wanted that. I want us to establish new traditions that Nicole remembers." So that's what we did. It's like we started a whole new life.

I became obsessed with solving the crime. I had to know whether I had done the right thing. Did I contribute to my mother's murder by moving her into a "safe" neighborhood? Would she still be alive if I hadn't? I don't think she really wanted to move, but she consented because she knew it would make me happy. I had to answer the question, "Was it something I did that contributed to her death?"

As an engineer, I'm a control freak. I tend to feel like nothing is impossible to solve. So when

I would call law enforcement and they couldn't give me an answer, that was unacceptable to me. I literally conducted the investigation myself in many ways. I would sit there all day long, piecing together the little pieces of information that I had. I had to have something that would help me focus my energies in areas that I could understand so I wouldn't go nuts. That's the way it was for six years.

I was going nowhere very fast. I became so disillusioned that I couldn't solve the problem that I began to have suicidal thoughts. Then I spoke with a friend of mine who said, "If you give up, they will win." I thought, "Damn it, that's right!" That's all I needed. Now I had a new purpose for staying on the problem.

The crime was solved fairly recently because of my tenacity and the assistance of the victim services director. I finally convinced the right people to go back and perform the investigation the way it should have been done. That was my turning point; I felt I was getting control again. Something in my life was solved. I now had some answers that provided me some solace or relief.

Once the crime was solved, I thought, "What do I do now?" My mind is clear all of a sudden. I'm not thinking of what happened to Mom that night. Now I have two focuses. I'm trying to get a statewide "cold case" squad at the Department of Public Safety. This would have the latest technology and provide a statewide resource so that if law enforcement really wanted to solve an unsolved crime, they could call in this office. The other focus is that I want to get the certification required for criminal investigators.

Before, I thought that the criminal justice system worked. I now know that is it broken. It has so much need for change and repair that somebody needs to do it. I'm willing to take a shot at certain parts of it.

— Vincent Torres

# "It affects you viscerally. You're on the floor with it; you're incapacitated."

I had been a musician all my life. Music is what I lived and breathed and ate and drank. After Noah's death, music was devastating. Now it's no longer something that motivates me. It's been replaced by my intellectual endeavor to find out why things are wrong and how to correct them. My son can't die and not have the world become different for somebody else.

When we were notified that, as parents of a murdered child, we weren't considered victims of crime by the criminal injury compensation board, I became very angry. On that same weekend, we found out that the guy who killed my son had been released from jail. He spent about a year and a half in jail for murdering my son.

He was 20 or 21 when he killed Noah, and I had come to realize that if he were to spend 10 or 15 years in jail, it would do nothing but victimize him. He pled guilty to criminal negligence causing death and was given three years. I thought the judgment was fair because I didn't want another life to be wasted. But when I found out that lawyers had been hired to overturn his sentence, and that they got away with doing that, my anger and frustration were incredible. We had not been informed of the sentencing review hearing and therefore had no input.

I spent every day talking to politicians and justice people. Eventually five families of murder victims came together, and we lobbied to get the criminal injury act interpreted fairly and justly. We were about to go to a Supreme Court hearing when the government amended the legislation to make it explicit that family members of murder victims are victims of crime.

A tragedy like this affects you viscerally. You're on the floor with it; you're incapacitated. The offender has to participate in that somehow. He also needs to be on the floor with it. There is no way to heal without confronting the

KEITH KEMP

*The process of recovery for me was in large part brought about by my having an effect on what was wrong with the justice system. Noah's death can't be in vain; he can't have died for nothing. Otherwise, the world doesn't make sense.*

issue, and that goes for the offender as well as the victim.

I have circulated a proposal for "transformational intervention" in the correction of offenders. Our justice system warehouses offenders and doesn't give them an opportunity to be at one with their deeds, with the consequences of their deeds, and with the persons they've harmed.

I believe that public safety can be achieved by the corrections system if offenders appreciate and share in the depth of pain and loss they have caused. It may be through ritual as in aboriginal cultures or through contact with the victim or surrogate victim. Unless you want more and more crime, you'd best make sure that the offender has every opportunity to know how horrible he has made life for others.

If there is any word that fits what I'm talking about, it's *atonement*. It is the concept on which I base many of my ideas about justice reform. *Compassion* is another. It comes from Latin, and literally it means "to suffer with." It's coming to a realization of the humanity that you share with the person that you hurt or injured. Somehow compassion must be introduced into the offender's experience.

People shouldn't go to prison so they can suffer. The suffering they need to do is to share the suffering they've inflicted. I would also like it to be known that there are far worse places than prison. Being the parent of a murder victim is a much worse place than being inside any restrictive environment. (A mother of a murdered son asked me a few months ago, "Would you rather be the parent of a murdered child or the parent of a murderer?" That's a very heavy question to ponder!)

We need to get a sense that we're all on one planet, and unless we stop destroying it, we're not going to reach the compassion that we need in order to endure the suffering. There are an awful lot of lies being told by people who have too much power concentrated in too few hands. Ultimately, as a result, there is more suffering going on than there needs to be.

I grew up believing that you can achieve more through cooperation than by competing. If there are two people on an island, one of them is not going to survive without the other. In a nutshell, that is the basis upon which we all have to reconcile our lives.

— Keith Kemp

*People shouldn't go to prison*
*so they can suffer.*
*The suffering they need to do*
*is to share the suffering*
*they've inflicted.*

# "I've had some anger that one of the offenders walked."

I grew up not being certain who my real father was. But when my father died of a heart attack, we went to a house in North Philadelphia where he had lived. When I walked in, the first person I saw was a guy who looked just like me. My father had been a big-time drug dealer, and my brother was my father's enforcer. I was 19 and had never met my brother until then. After my father's death, my brother started using drugs and losing respect. Within five years he was murdered over $10 that he owed somebody.

I was brought up totally different than my brother and knew right from wrong. So I knew I didn't want to be involved in that part of my brother's life. But my brother and I became close. It was like, "I have a brother!" In spite of his wrongs, I saw him as a human being. And he was real proud of me.

I work in victim services in the district attorney's office. The day after my brother was mur-dered, I came to work and on my desk was a file with his name on it. The ironic thing is that I wasn't even notified of my brother's murder trial, because everyone assumed that I would know since I'm in the homicide unit!

I see my work in victim services as a way to give something back to the community. Since I'm from the streets, I think I have enough credibility to someday develop a program to provide more help to families in these situations. I want to make sure that no more co-victims of homicide experience the re-victimization that I went through. I tell families I work with that I am also a co-victim of homicide. I'm professional, but I have a heart.

I am dedicated to making a positive contribution to the inner city. I felt that way before my brother's death, and since then it has been more highlighted for me. It has been more imprinted on my heart that I cannot give in to temptations to make the fast dollar or be influenced by life on the streets.

**LELAND KENT**

*I've had some anger that one of the offenders walked. I work in the system. I can find where they hang out, so if I didn't have convictions, I would take justice into my own hands. But I would be no better than they are. And I have a family—a son, a wife, a mother. I have too much to live for.*

The experience did make me angry at the system, but I don't believe that you can make a change from outside the system. I'm not burnt out. I'm actually rejuvenated every day when I can talk to a mother on the phone and help her through a crisis, help her understand that it was not her fault that her child caught a bullet that was meant for somebody else. I get joy out of helping people when they are most vulnerable because I've been there.

I don't want to meet with my brother's killers. They have never admitted it, never said, "We're sorry." If I were to meet with them and they were still cocky, that would make me more angry. I pray that they have learned from the experience and will not be repeat offenders.

I do want to work more with offenders though. I'm involved now in the Victim Offender Mediation Program here in Pennsylvania. In the next five years I would like to figure out a way where I can make a positive influence on those who are still in the world of the lost. Offenders make a ripple in someone's life, but have no clue about the damage they've done. And their lives mean nothing to the criminal justice system either.

When I go into the courtroom, I see two sets of victims. The families of offenders are often victims, too. Sometimes they are hostile and want revenge. So I am in the middle, I am the liaison, and I enjoy my job. It's not about the money. It's about being able to go home and sleep and be at peace.

I can't change my brother's life, but I can change his children's lives. I can change my son's life. I can be a real father to him, and to the second child that is on the way. That's the most important thing to me.

— Leland Kent

*Offenders make a ripple in someone's life,*
*but have no clue about the damage they've done.*
*And their lives mean nothing*
*to the criminal justice system either.*

# "All of a sudden you realize you're not in control."

*Juan:* On July 1st, 1997 my son Juan Javier and a young woman he was visiting were carjacked by two 17-year-old men. I have a hard time calling them men—they're children. Juan negotiated with them to let the young woman go. They tied her to a tree, then drove around with Juan. They bumped into another car and carjacked that driver. Finally, they tied up both of them, put them in the trunk of the car, and pushed the car into a lake.

The two men were arrested and confessed. They each accepted two 40-year life sentences. We were relieved. We really didn't want the death penalty. Juan was very much against the death penalty and so were we.

Juan had just finished his bachelor's degree. He wanted to go into politics because, he said, "I like working with people, and I think that's the best way to make a difference." Martha said, "You'll have to go to law school," and he replied, "No, we have too many lawyers in politics. We need historians."

*Martha:* We had worked all our lives to make this city responsive to everybody. We hoped that Juan would be the one to continue our work. I guess one frustration is that all of a sudden, when we were ready to take it easy, we find ourselves kind of burdened with his life, his continuity.

*Juan:* It's such a difficult thing to raise children. You never know if you are doing the right thing. When you can finally settle in and relax and deal with them on an equal basis, it's very nice. We had very much a relationship between friends. I miss that a great deal.

*Martha:* Juan and Juan Javier had such a wonderful relationship. It was a tremendous source of joy to see how much they loved each other.

*Juan:* I've always tended to feel I was in control. I could solve problems for my family. As an architect, I've spent my life negotiating things, and

JUAN AND MARTHA COTERA

*The measure of our civilization is not technology, but our attitude about life and how we treat each other. The abhorrence of violence is certainly a measure of how civilized we are. We're not very civilized because we still solve our problems with violence.*

always carrying a feeling that I have control. I can walk away from negotiations. I can make a decision. All of a sudden you realize you're not in control, that things can happen and there's no way to solve them. All you can do is accept what's going on. That's a bit of a shock. It reminded me that the universe and reality are really chaos, and there's nothing you can do about it.

I had enormous anger like I had never felt before. You realize you could be as violent as anybody else if you allowed yourself to be. The difficulty is that you don't know how to direct the anger. The only way I could explain it was that I was really angry with God.

*Martha*: One time I said, "Juan, be careful. God is not going to forgive these angry words." He said, "The question is will I ever forgive God!"

*Juan*: I was angry because it would have been easy to trade places. I was 60 and I've lived a good life. It wouldn't have been a difficult choice to say, "No, take me." But of course you don't get that chance.

*Martha*: Early on I made Juan promise when he was really emotional that he would see a therapist, that we would see a therapist together as long as we needed to.

*Juan*: Of course I was convinced I didn't need to. It's not that I didn't want to go, but all the psychologists and psychiatrists I know are totally nuts. I said, "Look, I want somebody that's stable, who has managed their own problems." So

Martha found a very nice person. It was not threatening and I was able to talk a lot, and to talk with Martha. In retrospect, I think it did me a lot of good.

*Martha*: Juan sat through all the hearings. Somehow I never seemed to know when they were going to happen. I got really angry; I did not need to be protected. I felt it was sexist that he wouldn't tell me. The counselor helped me understand that Juan was not doing it as a put-down, but that he was trying to protect me. I came to peace with it. I said, "I can love Juan for it instead of being resentful of him." Therapy is so absolutely necessary!

*Juan*: I didn't see the sentencing phase of the trial as closure. You have an enormous feeling of wanting to understand and not being able to. Something in me wants to talk to the two young men. I don't think I can yet, but eventually I want to. I'm convinced they don't know why they did what they did. If I could see some understanding on their part of what they've done, an acceptance of responsibility, a wish to do something with their lives that could go toward making up for that—I would feel closure.

I'm not sure I agree with 80 years in prison, because they're going to die in prison. That certainly doesn't do me any good, and it doesn't do Juan any good. I wasn't ready to put them back on the streets by any means, but I wish there were a way to institutionalize them until they understood what they've done—understood the moral implications of what they've done, and what they've done to humanity. That's the kind of institution I'd like to see, not just for these two young men, but for anybody that acts against society.

When you saw these kids at the hearing, they were pitiful. I believe they acted out something they had seen in the movies—the way they held their guns, a kind of swagger. How can you get angry with these kids because something allowed them to have a gun in their hands and something allowed them to feel powerless? I'm not saying they shouldn't be punished, although I don't know if *punished* is the right word.

We have a state that solves its problems by killing. We don't know what else to do. Well, there are many solutions other than killing. But everybody's biggest role model, the state, tells us the way we solve certain problems is to kill people. If society can do it, why can't I do it? I can't help but think that's one of the basic instigators of violence.

*Martha*: I have horrible anger toward the system. That's where the real evil is. The real evil is politicians who answer a real human need with pablum—people that divert our money toward uses other than resolving horrible human problems. The disregard for people's needs represents another face of violence.

*Juan*: I tried to figure out one day what Juan's death had cost, the total cost. You have to figure the fact that Juan's not around to do whatever good he might have done for society, that the other young man died, that we've incarcerated

two people, that Martha and I have had losses in professional productivity, that our friends experienced this loss as well. If you take all this into account, how can a program be too expensive? It's insane, what we keep doing.

*Martha*: I think it's the devaluation of life in this society that is so awesome, especially in regard to minority youths. You can't devalue their lives, then expect them to respect the lives of others.

The youths were African Americans and that complicates things for me, but it's very understandable. We forget to acknowledge our society's institutionalized racism against blacks; horrendous violence was instituted during slavery. I'm angry that we were victimized by our own society, not just by the boys themselves. Our loss was a direct result of that violent institution's aftermath. So my anger goes to the core of the problem.

*Juan*: People ask me why we should deal a little differently with minorities. They say, "Look at you. You did fine and you're a minority." I didn't know I had a choice. In my home, you were going to finish high school and you were going to college. There was no choice. There were no bars set up, nothing to stop me. Most minority kids don't have a tradition in the family of going to college. It's just not something they consider.

*Martha*: This is supposed to be a progressive city, but minority kids don't get the kinds of jobs that allow them to make good money and go to school.

*Juan*: There was a workshop recently on the causes of violence. It was a surprise to me to learn that we understand the causes of violence. We know what the solutions are. But there's not the political will to implement them.

*Martha*: At the funeral, someone said, "We'll start a memorial fund." Before we knew it, we had $40,000. Now we have established a foundation to work at prevention.

Juan wanted us to get going on it right away, but I was not ready. I wanted to make sure about our feelings before we did anything. I didn't want it to be something to help us heal. If it's primarily a part of our healing process, then what happens when we heal? Do we dump the whole thing? I want it to be something to accomplish the ends that Juan Javier wanted, to teach kids to never consider violence as a means to anything. It's been a little over two years, and I think now we're ready to do something this spring.

*Juan*: The only thing that's left after something like this is relationships and friendships. You value those more and that improves life. I have a great deal of interest in people and humanity. As vicious and mean as they can be, they can also be sublime in what they do. The city just drew together. Their reaction was very good, and I've appreciated that.

— Juan and Martha Cotera

*Martha* : Our granddog Sophie was a victim, too. She was raised by our son from when she was a little puppy. So she was very, very close to him and was very depressed after his death.

The day of the funeral we were in Juan's old room and Sophie was there, just moping around. All of a sudden she started jumping like she used to do. My son would hold up bacon bits and make her jump really high. She did that several times, all alone. And we were just too stunned to say anything. Then after jumping around a few times, she sat and looked toward the window with a very fixed stare.

I was in the kitchen on the morning before my daughter's wedding a year and a half later, and I felt something watching me. I turned back, and there was a tiny bird on the floor looking at me. Sophie was in the doorway looking at the bird, never making a move toward it, which is really odd for her.

I said to my daughter, "Come over here. There's a bird in here. I can't understand how it got in." We didn't have the doors open. The little birdie didn't try to fly out; it just hopped, hopped, hopped all the way to Juan's room. The bird stood there staring at us on the floor. Sophie was not tensing at all and the bird was not afraid of Sophie. It came practically up to her nose.

And then we let the birdie go into Juan's bedroom. There was a sculpture on the bed and the bird just stood on top of its head. It was the funniest thing. Maria and I began talking to it: "Well, do you want to go out? What do you want to do?" Sophie wouldn't make a move toward it. She just stood there in the middle of the floor.

Then we opened the window. I had a pillow over a toy chest, and the little birdie landed on the pillow and sat there for the longest time, looking at me, looking around. Then I said, "I wonder if I can pet you a little bit, just once." And I petted its little wings. Then it just flew out. Isn't that amazing? I said, "I'm not going to say anything about this because people will think I'm cuckoo." But it was incredible.

*Juan:* Martha and my daughter get upset because I'm the unbeliever. I pooh-pooh all these things.

— *Martha and Juan Cotera*

99

"We grabbed onto
all sorts of things as we were falling . . .
One of these was forgiveness."

# "Rage—that's hate with a lot of chili sauce poured on it."

When I was young and in college, I joined demonstrations against the death penalty. Now I'm proud that my native state of Texas is number one in capital punishment.

Something personal happened to totally change my mind. My 76-year-old mother was murdered on July 18th, 1976, while she was getting ready to go to church. Ronnie Wayne tortured her for several hours before finally finishing with this saintly old woman by stomping her to death with his cowboy boots.

Her murder was absolutely devastating. There's not one day since it happened that I don't think about it. Rage—that's hate with a lot of chili sauce poured on it.

I don't think of myself as good old Charley Nipp. I know I've got the same depth of evil as that Ronnie Wayne son of a bitch does. Everybody has a demon caged up that he can let go. But I haven't let mine go. It's your own choice to do what you do. So I've become more conservative because of this, conservative in the sense of responsibility for myself.

I have campaigned to have parole laws changed, and I have been able to have this man registered as a sex offender. And I'm a gun nut now. I don't know if that has anything to do with my mother's death, but my interest has become much more pronounced since then.

I'm a devoted Catholic, and Jesus tells me I have to forgive. I've made the decision to forgive, but the emotion doesn't seem to have followed. My priest says, "The fact that you made the decision means you have forgiven him as far as God is concerned. Any emotion you get out of it has to come from God." God doesn't seem to have given me much of that yet.

That choice to forgive is a daily thing. I have to forgive every day or I lose it. It'd be real easy for me to go back to hating him as much as I used to, which is a lot worse than now, believe

CHARLES E. NIPP

*I understand myself better because of this. It's peeling me like an onion. But if you keep peeling an onion, you don't have anything left. It hasn't gotten down that far yet—I'm still peeling.*

me. But I don't think I'll ever feel a warm rush of love for Ronnie Wayne Lawrence!

Our duty in life is to become perfect in the sense of *completed*. I don't know what *perfect* is, but I haven't reached it yet. Thank God we Catholics got purgatory and don't have to choose between heaven and hell! I'm shooting for purgatory because there's no way I'm going straight to heaven.

I find the church very helpful and I read my Bible. I still get mad at God oftentimes, but he can take it. I do have a lot of questions I'm going to ask God when I get there, and I've got a lot of suggestions I could give!

If I were God, there are a lot of things I would do differently. I would zap everybody and just leave the good folks. If I'd been in charge from the beginning, I think I would have gone ahead and gotten rid of the human race pretty quickly. It was a big mistake!

But I'm still learning. Eventually I'm going to have my meeting with Ronnie Wayne Lawrence, one of those supervised meetings put on by the Texas department of corrections. I just want to talk to him. I just want to listen to him, to see what comes out. I think he will bullshit and cover everything up. Maybe he won't—he's already confessed—but I'd just like to see what he says. I don't have great hopes.

— Charles E. Nipp

*That choice to forgive is a daily thing.*
*I have to forgive every day*
*or I lose it.*

# "I couldn't park my angers, my fears."

One day in 1985 my ex-wife's husband marched over to her apartment and held three people hostage—my ex-wife and my little son and daughter. The local RCMP (police) detachment surrounded the building, but even though they had telephone negotiations with the man, they couldn't help. He just destroyed them— shot all three of them, put the gun down on the kitchen table, gave himself up to police.

A couple of years after the murders, I was searching. I had gone to a therapist. I had some religious experiences. It gave me some temporary relief, I think, because we were avoiding the issue. But I had to find out why this guy had done what he did, to understand. One day I made a call to his mother and she said, "Would you like my son to write to you?" I said, "Yes." Two weeks later I got a letter from him.

Nobody was there for us as a mediator or a gatekeeper. We just let the correspondence happen. I asked a lot of questions and we were able to communicate. And his apologies helped. It felt like a healing journey. It seemed that all my fears were taken care of. I had a nice relationship developing with this man. I parked my anger somewhere. There was peace.

But with more information, and as I got to know him better, I realized that it wasn't over. I couldn't park my anger, my fears. It wasn't that easy.

I visited him a couple of years after we started corresponding. It went fairly well. But after that meeting I discovered a book of interviews with murderers, and one of the interviews was with him. He admitted to the interviewer that he had sexually molested my daughter. And I found out that he had beaten my ex-wife.

After he discovered that I had the book, he came up with a full confession about a sexual incident with my daughter that occurred four years before her death. That brought to the sur-

**JAMES KOSTELNIUK**

*Soon after the murders, I was taking a walk along the beach. The world was tilting, swaying out of proportion, and I realized that I wasn't the same psychologically or spiritually. Since that day it's definitely a different world than I knew. I've gone beyond my limits, way out where I've never been. But I'm still hopeful. I'm not defeated.*

107

face that maybe he hadn't been honest. He was twisting my arm, trying to persuade me not to make public that information. Now he's denying all this, so the whole story has changed again.

I sensed what his agenda was: get out of jail, obliterate this record, re-invent himself. So I had an extra burden that shouldn't have been mine, just because I have the information. I have to do something with it—either hide it or make it public. That is my burden.

I had done a lot of work on a book manuscript when I found out about his additional crimes and cover-ups. Now I had the problem of deciding what to do with the information, and so my writing stopped and the book went on the shelf. I tried to purge what I had learned, to turn my back on it. I wanted to run away from it all, but after four years I found that I couldn't quit writing. It's almost like destiny. My only option is to reveal the truth as I see it.[1]

I can't get around this man. He continues to have a central role in my life. My way of dealing with it is to tell *my* story. The book is a way of arranging things, of putting them into perspective. I've never done anything so difficult. There's some deep satisfaction about it, but also something very challenging. I guess it's because it's so close to the bone. It's about my blood, my feelings. But writing about things is a way of understanding. It's about meaning. In a way, I'm trying to reclaim the dead. Now that I've finished the book, I feel that I have accomplished something. It's my history, my story.

I don't know where exactly I am on this journey of mine, but I know I've gone beyond my limits. I don't know whether I'll be punished for that. What's the Greek word for going against the gods, for assuming too much? Hubris. And who was it that said, "Go sin boldly"? I've always been a conservative person, playing it safe. But this murder, and all the choices I have made since, has made me willing to do things that are unsafe because I think they have to be done. I feel a kind of moral courage because of it.

It's a morality play that I'm involved in. Are you going to forgive, or are you gonna kill the guy? Is he going to kill you to protect himself? And then there's the question of forgiveness. At some point, I guess, you have to decide what action you're going to take.

Forgive. That's the first thing you're supposed to do. People from church told me that. I didn't know what they meant. It offended me, that I should forgive and get over it. And it didn't happen. I tried forgiveness. I did try, very hard, and for a while it worked. It made me feel good.

I tried to make a deal with the killer—that he would lay down his gun and I would lay down mine (even if it was a symbolic one), that we could make peace and go on living. But even though it seemed to be working at the time, it really hasn't materialized.

Now I believe that there are some things you can't forgive. I don't know if God can forgive them. And forgiveness is irrelevant anyway, because the only people that have that right or ability are the dead. We assume we have the power to forgive. But in those situations where a kin is killed, you don't really. The survivor doesn't have that right. I don't have that right.

When victims talk about forgiveness, I think they wish they could take a shortcut and put it behind them. It's like saying, "Okay, you owe me a hundred bucks? And you can't pay me? Okay, I'll write it off." And then you can just walk away from this guy that you don't like anyway. I find the whole concept rather hollow, even though I participated, or tried to. It didn't seem to do him any good. Didn't do me any good.

I explained my forgiveness to him like this. Prior to our negotiations and his asking for forgiveness and my forgiving him, there was a rope between us and we were having a tug of war. It isn't very healthy to be fighting in a tug of war your whole life. I wanted to forgive and to let go of the rope so that he could go his way and I could go mine. He wandered on his journey, but do you know what? The rope is still there. There's still the tug of war. We haven't escaped that metaphor.

When I first started on this journey I wanted to help other people. My wife, Marge, and I set up a victim's group. But I was the one who really needed help the most. The main thing that I found out is that I've got this big wound here, close to my heart, that won't heal. And the wind blows through there.

It's been a spiritual journey because it started out that way. As a small child, I believed in God. I saw God in the sun, the stars, the prairie fires. Then when I was about 13 my parents became Jehovah's Witnesses and I went with them. The Jehovah's Witness experience for me was negative in the long run. I asked questions and, because they were never answered, I left and I paid the price. I was dis-fellowshipped and lost my family. But I still had some sort of feeling of the presence of God.

Then came the murders and I began to question God. It seemed that he was an impotent tin-soldier God. The old deals that you make with God don't work: "I'll be this good Christian, I'll go to church, I'll preach for you. Therefore you're gonna give me this nice life." It doesn't work that way. You can't make deals with God.

My concept of God has totally changed. I don't see him as a person I can talk to. There's a presence. I feel the presence. But outside of that I really don't know anything. I'm spiritually illiterate. That feels more human. It humbles you. You can't make deals with this being, can't twist his arm, can't get what you want. You have to accept that.

The meaning of life? I've learned that I don't have nearly as much control as I thought I had, that most of the controls are in the cosmos, beyond me. That is a good thing to learn. It's very useful, but it's not something we want to know. And we delude ourselves into thinking we have more control. Maybe this lesson is a part of getting older, too.

— James Kostelniuk

[1] Jim's book, *Wolves Among Sheep: The True Story of Murder in a Jehovah's Witness Community,* was published by HarperCollins of Canada in 2000.

I just finished reading *The Old Man and the Sea*, Hemingway's book.

You remember—a Cuban fisherman goes out. He's an old man. He's had bad luck for 83 days. Nobody wants to have anything to do with him because he can't catch anything. So one day he goes out by himself in this little skiff. He goes beyond where fishermen normally go, into the night, and he hooks something. It is so big. No one would be able to hang on to a fish that big. But he holds on. Three days this fish is pulling him out to sea. He finally tires the fish out and he kills it.

He lashes the fish to his skiff—it is longer than the skiff—and comes back to Havana. The sharks start to attack the fish and they get the better half of it. At that point he's making deals with God. He says to God, "I'll say my 'Hail Mary's,' at least 100 of them. I'll go to church. I'll do anything. Just let me keep the other half of this fish. Otherwise there's no meaning to what I did. It's all in vain."

Then he starts thinking of sin. Maybe he's sinned because he went beyond his limits, where he shouldn't have gone. He knows that the sharks will come back and there will be nothing left but a skeleton. And he concludes that he's squandered his luck. He's violated it by going beyond his limits.

I feel that I've gone beyond my limits, way beyond. And I don't know what that means. I don't know whether I've sinned. I'm not smart enough to know what sin is. I do really feel just like that fisherman—that I've gone way beyond my limits, followed this thing way out to sea where there is nothing but birds, fish, and water. Now I'm trying to come back in with a skeleton.

The only good thing about the ending of the book is that the old man is finally validated because he's undefeated. In one way, he's defeated, but not in another. He's held in esteem by his fellow fishermen because at least they can see the skeleton that he brought. He had the courage to do that—to catch the fish, to bring it back, to fight the sharks. And because he's still alive, he's not totally defeated. I haven't come back yet. I'm still fighting sharks.

— James Kostelniuk

*I've always been a conservative person,*
*playing it safe.*
*But this murder, and all the choices I have made since,*
*has made me willing to do things that are unsafe*
*because I think they have to be done.*
*I feel a kind of moral courage because of it.*

# "We're having a problem forgiving the judge and the system."

Our son was murdered in prison by another inmate. That's not the beginning, nor is it the end of the story.

Gerald spent the last five years of his life languishing in prison for a crime he was not guilty of. We stuck by him as a family, and finally his conviction was overturned. Our hopes were up; he was going to come home. The prosecutor had an opportunity to appeal and he was granted bail. But we couldn't afford to get him out. Then he was murdered.

We dealt with so much anger at a system that would do this to us as a family. I'm still angry about it. I can't pretend that I'm not.

We never expected Gerald to be convicted in the first place, so we deal with the guilt of being naive. The evidence was just so flimsy. There was only one witness. Looking back we can see that she was a reluctant 16 year-old, up there telling a story she didn't want to be telling. Eventually she came forward and said that she lied, and told us why.

We're at the place of being able to forgive the girl who testified. But it is harder for us to forgive the system and some of the people in it.

There was the judge who sent our son to prison for life on the goofy testimony of a frightened young girl. That judge is now the District Attorney. She was running for D.A. when Gerald's case came up, so our son was a political casualty. He was someone to stomp on on her way to some other office, to show everybody how tough she was. And the prosecutor knew how to make us cry when he wanted to. The judge and the prosecuting attorney did not care about us. They just wanted a win.

You're caught up in a situation where you have no control. Even if someone is asking you questions, they're asking you because they want your answers to coincide with what they want. The prosecutor is trying to keep you fired

CONRAD MOORE

*We've talked to the man who murdered Gerald and have had an opportunity to extend forgive-ness to him, directly, right in the face. We're forgiving the frightened young girl, the only witness. She came forward and said she had lied. But we're having a problem forgiving the judge and the system.*

up and angry so that you testify well. They don't want healing to begin, because when you come to court, you still have to be angry and grieving.

Nobody in the system has ever said they're sorry. As a matter of fact, the people who represent the system were just so indifferent. It was monumental indifference. When we went to pick up Gerald's things after he was murdered, the warden never came out of his office. So, on the one hand, we're experiencing this monumental insensitivity and, on the other, they're using us to convict this guy.

Part of what made it more difficult for us is that my son was an African American male. I've been where my son was. I've been arrested, tried, and convicted as a teenager for a crime that I did not commit. As a person of color, you realize that this can happen to you, although you still don't quite expect it. You do expect to be harassed by the police. When you're a little boy, you're a cute little black boy, even to European Americans. But then after you start growing some facial hair, all of a sudden the cuteness goes away. It's replaced by a target; it's like having a bull's-eye. The police keep shooting at this target until they get you. It starts early. The police begin pulling you over, taking your name, and you've never done anything.

One of the ways I'm handling my grief is by staying busy and doing something about it, even if it's not something that's going to benefit Gerald. That's why I'm involved in racism awareness work, because racism played a huge role in this.

I'm getting so much satisfaction because I'm not only trying to put my life back in order, but I'm trying to spread out what I've learned beyond myself, beyond my family. I'm trying not to be naive enough to think that the system is going to change all of a sudden because of what I'm doing. But I am having little victories, just creating in certain little pockets an awareness that wasn't there before. I feel good about that.

My wife Teresa and I handle our grief differently. Most important is that we're able to talk about what's happening. When you aren't handling things well, somebody needs to pull you up and tell you that. We're able to do that with one another as a family. It's not always easy.

Gerald's murder was a real turning point for the family. It forced us to be real deliberate about talking about stuff. Like Teresa, for instance: every year, at a certain time of the year, she starts going through this crazy stuff. From March to July and around Gerald's birth—that's the dark zone. So we're real deliberate about naming and dealing with what we're facing—"We're in this time period. This is where it could happen. What are we going to do to address this?"

Families who go through such an experience have an astronomical divorce rate. I am determined that is not going to happen to us; I'm not gonna be in that statistic. The system has already had too much effect on this family, and I don't want to continue to give it power. I feel pretty good that my family has been able to continue to work through this stuff. We've had some times that could really have shaken the foundation of our family and our relationships, but we're both really determined. That's another way the anger plays out—we refuse to be part of that statistic.

I learned to journal after I became a Christian. Just writing for the sake of writing. Just spelling it out. I really need to do that, to just pour it out. Getting it out clears your mind. Not getting it out is like being constipated.

I've also learned to be more emotionally expressive. It helps me to identify what's going on within me. Am I hurt? Am I afraid? I had incredible hurt, and it expressed itself as anger. And I felt inadequate, unable to comfort my family. This grief was the biggest thing this family has ever experienced and, Conrad, you can't solve it. I knew it the night Gerald was murdered when I heard Teresa wailing. I've never heard that kind of wailing. It was like somebody had a knife. There's no way to describe how deep an agony it was. What do you do? What do you say? There's nothing to say. You just have to be there.

No family should have to go through this.

Forgiving was our only opportunity to exercise control in the whole process. When you forgive, you actually have some power. It's like a sign of relief.

God tells us to forgive. But when we started talking about forgiveness, it was not so much because we wanted to free the guy; it was mainly for ourselves. We didn't want to be consumed, and bitterness is so consuming. So we've been on a journey beyond this hate and bitterness.

As Christians, we believe that if people ask God's forgiveness, they will get it. So you're wasting your years being angry at a man who actually could be standing beside you in heaven because God forgave him!

Forgiveness is an act of will. You make the decision to forgive, and then the feelings come later. It's not always easy, and it is something that you do over and over and over. You have to remember that you're not forgiving because you're trying to be religious, but because you need to do this for you, so that your life can move on. If you want to bring any honor to the life of the person who was murdered or hurt, the best way to do that is to be made a better person yourself. The healing process cannot be tied to the punishment of the perpetrator, because when you do that, you devalue your loved one.

Even though it's been five years, I don't think we're done by any means. It's not like we went to counseling and it's all fixed. *Recovery* is the right word to use. I would place myself still in recovery.

— Conrad Moore

# "We were free-falling into a dark abyss, frantic to find footholds."

We were an ordinary family with three kids. It was an ordinary day in 1984, payday, and 13-year-old Candace didn't come home from school. For six and a half weeks we looked for her. Then, on January 17th, her body was found in a shack with her hands and feet tied. She died of exposure. The police still haven't shut the case and it is still on the unsolved mystery list. I saw it on TV just this week.

It changed our lives. We have a B.C. and an A.C.—before Candace and after Candace. But when I see her on TV, I don't go into trauma anymore. She is still part of our lives, and I'm privileged that she's still remembered.

Even though the killer has never been found, I think I have experienced justice, and that was a real surprise for me. Justice is, for the lack of better words, the healing of the soul. Certain components have to happen for justice to take place. We as victims need truth, judgment of the wrongdoing, validation, and vindication.

I used to think that these things needed to happen in the courtroom and I yearned for that. But after hearing other victims who had been to trial complain about not feeling that justice was served, I realize that a trial doesn't guarantee these things. In the end, we were spared the re-victimization of the criminal justice system.

My husband Cliff and I were forced to go with another kind of justice: finding truth by telling our story. I wrote a book—my story, my version. We were very fortunate in that our story was accepted, validated, and affirmed. Our community said very clearly that the murder of our daughter was wrong. By their actions, like building a swimming pool as a memorial for her, they told us that Candace was valued. They also gave her memory life. So there's a thing called creative justice that can happen outside the system. But it takes a lot of work!

**WILMA DERKSEN**

*Forgiveness is such a wonderful, comforting word when we are offenders—it can be a warm, cozy blanket word. But when we are victims, it's so hard because it's so costly.*

I think lament is an important part of this, but the anger and need for justice can suppress the need to just cry and go through the grief. Often homicide survivors are in fighting gear, and the person who died can get lost in the issues. We had a wonderful funeral. It was important for us to remember Candace and who she was, to dig out those memories and dissociate the Candace who froze in the shack from the Candace who lived with us. My book was a form of lament.

The experience was like being at the top of a cliff, and all of a sudden, somebody knocked my fingers off and we were free-falling into a dark abyss. We were frantic to find footholds that would not only give us justice but would preserve our family and our lives. This was a matter of survival. So we grabbed onto all sorts of things as we were falling, and we held on frantically. One of those things was forgiveness. That was a good thing, although the twig of forgiveness broke once or twice and we had to relearn what that meant.

For me, forgiveness is still a moving target, because as soon as I've got an understanding of it, it moves on me.

I think there are two levels of forgiveness. Right after our tragedy, my idea of forgiveness was to be free of this thing—the anger, the pain, the self-absorption. It was totally personal, a survival tactic to leave the experience behind. It had nothing to do with the offender. I still maintain that is a part of forgiveness—just letting go.

But the second level was realizing how the word forgiveness applies to the relationship between the victim and the offender. It means accepting and working on that relationship and making things right between two people. The latter is more complicated, and I haven't had that opportunity. But I have forgiven because I have integrated these experiences into my life in a controlled way, rather than just letting them go or escaping them.

Letting go and accepting has nothing to do with letting offenders off the hook. They need to be held accountable and feel the consequences of their actions. Just like victims need to suffer through the pain of their losses to heal, offenders also need to suffer through their guilt in order to heal. My holding them accountable is their way to freedom, too. Accountability is not a victim's vicious, vindictive agenda; it is a way that both of us can free ourselves.

Forgiveness involves wanting to understand what happened, dealing with it, and resolving it as best you can. I did that journey, but partly it was vicarious, through going to prison and talking to lifers. I was asking, "Why, why?" and saying, "It was wrong." But I didn't have to hold them accountable with my *words*. They saw it in my *presence*. Those interactions I've had with prisoners over the years were part of my forgiveness, too.

The twig of forgiveness helped in forgiving myself. I had tremendous guilt—and the what-ifs! Candace had called me to pick her up, but I was running late and said, "No, you walk home." I went through hell. Blame is a wild thing. It's usually a cousin of anger. Probably a lot of my anger came out of that guilt and my inner need for vindication.

I've changed my ideas about anger. Before, I saw anger as something that would destroy you, an enemy you needed to overcome. I now see that, yes, an anger that just stews and has no place to go is a killer. But anger is a natural response, and anger is a motivation to do something about injustice. I had every right to be angry that somebody took Candace. There's still a big stream of anger against injustice that I can tap into. I'm still a meek, mild, inhibited Mennonite girl, but if I kick into that anger, I can talk to anybody! It's an overriding energy that this injustice has got to stop.

Entrenched in my Mennonite heritage is a commitment to peace. But I know now that I could kill. I now understand where that desire to kill comes from. What I found in myself revolutionized my ideas of what human beings are like.

I had tremendous rage. But when I got in touch with my own violence, I also realized I didn't want to perpetrate "an eye for an eye," because, as the trite saying goes, everyone would be blind. It's got to stop. That's the mission of love—to be able to transcend our own hurts and create more love. Otherwise we're going to continue the cycle of violence.

God looks totally different from this side of the murder. I experienced a real destruction of the God I had known or wanted to believe in. He's not in total control; he's not a sugar daddy. It's a scary thought. I found that God looks for good things to bless, but he isn't about controlling things. God understands the value of suffering, the value of allowing good and evil to live together. For awhile I went through a deep abyss in my faith, but now I not only see the suffering, I see God's blessings also.

It was wonderful to realize God's son had been murdered. That crucifixion stuff was a comfort. I could really relate to all that darkness and then his rising. There's going to be hope somewhere. God is suffering, too. And we become better people because of the suffering. It's an awful philosophy, though. I don't want my children to suffer, yet I know that it's my suffering and my failures that have been the best teachers in my life.

I still think the essence of our life is loving and being able to transcend ourselves. We're incredibly selfish people, incredibly self-absorbed. Life always rewards any tiny effort that we make to transcend our own self-interest and to make somebody else's life a little better. Probably our suffering gives us some tools to do that.

— Wilma Derksen

Wilma Derksen helped begin the organization, Victims' Voices, 134 Plaza Dr. Winnipeg, MB, R3T 5K9, CANADA.

*"Shaking hands with Charles . . .*
*that's the hand that held the gun*
*that murdered my son."*

In a growing number of communities in the United States and Canada, victims who wish to do so are being offered an opportunity to meet with their offenders through a carefully structured process. Although this is sometimes termed victim-offender mediation, in cases of severe violence the process may be better termed victim-offender dialogue or conference.

# "Every time my life was getting back in order, he would appear on TV."

I was driving back to Houston from Baton Rouge, listening to a Christian radio station, and they were talking about forgiveness. I couldn't understand how God would expect me to forgive. I was nearly being eaten alive. But they were talking about how you have to be able to forgive to be able to go on. I knew what they were talking about because I was a walking dead person.

I'm driving down the interstate and I'm crying and saying, "Dear God, how can I forgive Jonathan for what he did?" And this voice was audible in the back of the car: "You don't have to forgive what he did; you have to forgive him." Something exploded my heart. I had to pull off the road, I was crying so hard. I don't know how long I sat there, but God just released everything right there in the car with that small statement.

My daughter Mitzi was murdered on her birthday in 1986, along with her roommate.

September 13th was Mitzi's birthday, and last year I had my meeting with Jonathan, the man who murdered her, on September 22nd. Two weeks after that, he was executed.

I felt that every time my life was kind of getting back in order, Jonathan would appear on TV trying something. I'd get a notice that his appeals were coming up, or he was trying to get a new trial because he was an abused child. The list goes on and on. My focal point was keeping him on death row. I couldn't bear the thought that someday he might be released.

I had also been trying to see him since the minute the trial was over because I wanted to talk to him. I really don't know why; I didn't know what I was going to say to him. But I couldn't get in.

Then in 1998, when someone from victim services asked me if I would like to participate in a new victim-offender mediation program, it was like God answered a prayer. We started

PAULA KURLAND

*It asks in the Bible, if you don't forgive, how can God forgive you? I felt that this was more than I could ever do. But when I did finally forgive Jonathan, I learned to forgive a lot of other people, too. Through forgiving Jonathan, I've learned to forgive everybody else. It just released me.*

preparation, and it was the most wonderful thing that's ever happened to me. That program literally gave me back my life.

The mediation was the hardest thing that I've ever had to do, second only to burying my child. It lasted five and a half hours and was a life-changing event. I got everything out; I was able to say everything that I felt I needed to say. Now there's a hole in my heart that will always be there, but it doesn't consume my heart anymore.

I wish the meeting hadn't been so close to the execution. I had wanted to witness the execution, but when I made that decision, it was because I wanted to be the last person he saw. I wanted him to see what he was leaving behind, what kind of pain he was leaving. After the mediation it was very difficult to watch the execution, because the man I spoke with was not the same man that I sat in the courtroom with for 13 months.

What Jonathan did was wrong, and he got the sentence he deserved, but it was very difficult to witness his death after he and I had come to terms with each other. He had become a Catholic and he left me a medal; it's called a miraculous medal. I carry it with me everywhere with my rosary beads.

It's so amazing what happens in the middle of all the things that go on after you've experienced a violent crime. God has a way of picking you up and putting you places that you would never dream of being, under any sort of circumstances. No one could have convinced me that I would be working in prisons today. I had to share that because I am very proud of that.

I walked out of the mediation on death row a different person. Before, I couldn't get involved in any kind of victims' movements, because how could I tell somebody else how to heal when I couldn't heal? After the mediation, I said I wanted to become active in victims' things. I didn't care about offenders, and I didn't want to talk to somebody else's offender. But people at victim services said, "Just give John Sage's victim-offender project a try.[1] Come and meet with victims who have participated in his project in prison."

So I went to orientation, and I heard victims talk about all the things that were happening between them and the offenders in the program. I was absolutely appalled that they wanted relationships with offenders. They were talking about loving those people. I thought they were sick. They started talking about hugging these guys good-bye. I said, "I'll give it a try, but I'm

It's hilarious. I did three of these projects in prison last year, and each lasted for 12 to 14 weeks from start to finish. And I stay in contact with most of those offenders. Isn't that amazing? I'm telling you, what happens in those circles is a miracle. What I see happening is that it is making a change in those offenders. It's healing for me. Every time I come out of there, I've grown by leaps and bounds.

I was at the very pit of the abyss when I got the news that my daughter had been murdered. That is the lowest that anybody could ever go. Now I'm as high as the heavens, and it's only because God has put me there. Now the sky is the limit. I'm still growing. My heart just expands every day.

— Paula Kurland

telling you right now, I don't want those people touching me. Don't let them come near me." Well, I went out there, and, needless to say, I bonded with two of them instantly—one black, one white. They're both out now, and I'm following up with them.

[1] Bridges To Life invites victims of violent crime into prison to interact during a 12-week program with inmate volunteers who are soon to be released.

# "It's like a twister coming through your house."

Seven years ago on Thanksgiving weekend my sister Jeanette was killed in a car accident, along with her girlfriend. It was drunk-driving, and the offender had a pattern of that. My sister and I were best friends.

It's like a twister coming through your house. You slowly have to clean up, fix the broken pieces, replace things. Eventually your home will become your home again. I had to pull myself up for my kids' sake. But for the first month I blacked out. I think it's by grace we are given this shock, this numbness. It's some sort of shield that God puts upon us to protect us those first couple of weeks.

I'm a take-charge person—my middle name is "Going"—so I had to take charge of my life. I was in control of my life, and I wasn't going to let this fellow take me down along with my sister. Since I can't counsel myself, I had to go find someone that would help me through. And I had to get in contact with the offender. I didn't have victim services tell me this, and I didn't know about such a program then. I had to go through all sorts of red tape to find it.

People thought I was crazy, but through the victim-offender mediation program I met with the offender in prison. I basically gave him a picture of Jeanette. I wanted him to see, hear, and feel my hurt and loss. I was hoping that maybe I could make a little bit of difference in his life.

But he still has a very cocky attitude about everything. He was feeling sorry for himself, concerned more about his son being born while he was in prison. I said, "Hello. I can't even be Jeanette's bridesmaid. I can't be there when she has her first baby."

I didn't like his attitude, and I don't think he really understood what he did, but I forgave him. I felt comfortable saying that to him, because to me, that was another step of healing. Who am I to judge? That's between him and

JOANNE VOGT

*You've just completed this beautiful puzzle. All of a sudden, someone comes along and just swishes it off the table and you have to start putting it back together. Then there's a piece missing that you just can't find anywhere. Your picture is completed, but there's a piece missing and you have to deal with that.*

127

God when it comes to judgment day. I did let him know, "I don't like what you did, and I don't like your attitude." There are still times I get upset with him, but a burden was lifted. Another part of my heart was healed. Talking with him was therapy for me.

My mom and dad are Canadian First Nations. They had a spiritualist come in and sweep their house with cedar branches to sweep away evil spirits. Then they had a "Thanksgiving dinner burning" for Jeanette, so that she could receive a Thanksgiving food plate sent up to her spirit world. I don't believe in that form of spirituality. I'm a Christian, the only one in my family, and I go by trust in God's written word.

I believe that God wasn't going to let me fall. He'd let me do the grief. He'd let me go through the mourning. He'd let me get angry, but I knew through all this, as foggy as it all seemed, he was there and would carry me through. Through my counselor I learned it's okay to be angry at God. It's better to be angry towards him than taking revenge or getting angry at the kids. I think it's only human for us to be angry at God.

The book of Job is all marked in my Bible. All the moaning and groaning, I can relate to that. And Psalms is one of my favorite books. That is a place where I can go. There is hope and praise and worship, but there are times when it is angry. I still go to it and read it over and over.

I've always been a butterfly person, just flapping my wings and going. Now I'm hoping to make a difference in people's lives. I've gotten involved in victim services because of what they gave to me when I lost Jeanette. I want to give that back. I'm hoping I can make a difference in someone's life, not by giving advice, but by walking through it with them, by being a leaning post.

— Joanne Vogt

*I had to pull myself up for my kids' sake.*
*But for the first month I blacked out.*
*I think it's by grace we are given this shock,*
*this numbness.*

# "I couldn't seem to feel good about myself."

If I were to write my story, I'd start when I met Dave and the rest of the victim-offender mediation group. That was when my life really started to turn around. Anything that happened before that is past, and everything from that day on is forward. After that I was able to embrace myself again and get rid of the ghosts of the past, to forgive and move on. There would be no end to this story. Life keeps getting better and better.

In 1978 I was sexually assaulted by a stranger. The case went through court proceedings and the offender basically got off. The trial itself was atrocious. I was interrogated and everything about me was on trial. The offender got off, and the next 20 years I lived with shame and guilt.

I hated him. I wanted him in prison to pay for what he did to me. I had so much fear in me that I could not hear his name without hyperventilating. I dreamed about him and what happened to me on a daily basis. This fellow's name is on a number of trucks. If I drove by a truck that had his name on it, I had to pull over and sit for awhile. I was paranoid and used to think that he was following me.

I couldn't relate well to men because of the assault. I had been married three months when this happened, and my marriage fell apart. I would put myself down. I became very much of an introvert. My professional growth was stunted. I had always been a motivated person at work, but now something held me back. I couldn't seem to get past certain things and feel good about myself.

Now I write to my offender who is in prison for a different offense. We don't write often, but I keep in touch. I don't even know why, except that I have developed a friendship out of it. Before I met Dave, there was no chance that I would ever have considered being on a speaking level with that person. That's the way I thought about him: that *person*.

DIANE MAGNUSON

*The letter itself—I distinctly remember the minute I read it. I had an incredible feeling, reading about this person I hated for so long. Before, I could have killed this man; I could literally have sat there with a gun and killed him for what he did. It wasn't just me he hurt; he hurt my father, my marriage. After the letter, I just felt so much peace.*

131

My first letter to him was a poem, because I could express myself better in poetry. My poem asked where he was at that minute, why he did what he did to me? He wrote back with a synopsis of his life and what brought him to that kind of anger. From that came an admittance of guilt as well, which I never got from him at the trial.

It was an immediate relief when he admitted his guilt and said he was sorry. I can still feel the overwhelming release of this sadness leaving me. At that moment, I think I forgave him. I felt a calming effect, an immediate release of sadness and anger and all those overwhelming emotions that go along with that.

He didn't go to jail for what he did to me, so he could have said, "Screw you. I don't need more hassles on my plate." So he actually had to sit down and think about what he did, and what it did to me, what his life was all about. I felt there was real sincerity in his letter, and I felt the pain he went through as a young boy growing into manhood.

It wasn't that what he did was okay. It was terrible what he did, but I now understood what led him to that. I understood that I was at the wrong place at the wrong time; it was nothing personal. It was his problem, not mine. I was able to put it in the past.

This does not end the accountability. He is in prison for a reason, although I'm not saying you should put a person in jail and throw away the key. I think people can change.

When you get rid of all the anger and other stuff, you can move on with your life. After my

first contact with him, it didn't take very long before I was moving up the ladder, feeling secure and confident. Now I'm a bank manager, I'm independent, I don't lack confidence, I feel good. I just don't think about that time in my life. I don't have nightmares anymore. I look younger now than I did eight or 10 years ago!

We have truly helped each other, and from that a bit of a bond has developed. But even if he had refused to do anything, the process would have helped me because it allowed me to put on paper my feelings and say, "This is yours; it belongs to you." It was good for me to go through the process, whether it was reciprocated or not. Maybe if it hadn't been, I wouldn't have come so far, but I would still have gotten rid of that sadness and anger and given it back to where it belonged. I think that my sitting down and writing the letter was very healing in itself. I released a lot of anger in that poem!

The only thing that is left unfinished in my life is that I would like to see him continue to grow. I need to know that he continues to develop and that he can lead a worthwhile life. This is a chance that makes my life even more worthwhile. We connected at one time with a lot of tension, and then at another time to sort of make amends. I'd like to know that he went forward from that.

I can't go back anymore and feel angry. That's proof that I've moved on. There's nothing left to feel angry about. I can think about that day and it doesn't bring any anger to my mind anymore. The fear is all gone. It's just something that happened.

There are amazing offshoots, really many side rivers, that flow from what happens to somebody. They take people's lives different routes, all because of one event. By being healed, all those things get changed, too.

— Diane Magnuson

# "You're always kind of looking over your shoulder."

Before and after—that's how I view things. I put events in those two columns and they don't cross over very easily.

My brother Randy was murdered in 1988 by a second cousin who is now serving a 10- to 20-year sentence. I had separated from my first husband and the murder pretty well finished things for me. I was dealing not only with the murder, but then the divorce and everything else.

I've had to take a lot of anger and capsulate it, shove it down and not do anything with it. Throw stuff and smash it—that's how I grew up. Through this, though, I am learning that it's okay to be mad, to not want to talk about it one day and to be overflowing with it the next. My husband has endured a lot!

On the day of the trial, I went to the cemetery and put a flower on Randy's grave and said, "We're going to nail him." When they brought back a verdict of third degree, I said, "We didn't do it!" He got third degree murder because he was drunk and didn't know what he was doing. He kind of got away with it. He's already had pre-release, and now we're dealing with impending paroles. We've had to go against him.

There's the security issue once he's out, especially since we live on a dairy farm off the road, back a farm lane. Once he's released, which is inevitable, we're probably going to go to wearing pagers or beepers or something. Even now we have an unlisted phone number and caller ID on the phone. I've got a 90-pound dog in the house.

We found out at his last parole hearing that his ex-wife lives less than two miles from my home, so we've withdrawn the kids from the school district, too. You're always kind of looking over your shoulder.

I promised Randy on the first day of the trial that I would confront his killer. I want to take pictures of Randy to the prison and say, "Now, this is who he was. Here's the picture of his tomb-

**SANDY HOUTZ**

*I used to get mad that my husband could escape from me and my problems by going to the barn. That's real fair—run to the barn and talk to the cows! I didn't have an escape. So he got me a donkey. The donkey's my project. It filled my downtime away from fussing kids. If I'm in a bad mood, that donkey is not going to do anything.*

135

stone. This is what you've left us with." He needs to understand the impact of what he has done. A primary question is "Why?!" And I don't want to live in a cage, so I want to know where his mind is now. Earlier he made threats. I'm hoping to see changes within him that will reassure me that I'll never have to be afraid of him again.

I also have to physically confront this person, to tell him I forgive him but I haven't forgotten. I've turned this over to God and given this guy forgiveness. That's the best thing I did. Before, I felt like I was dragging a rock around on my ankle all the time. It was like he was holding the keys to everything. But I want to see him on his knees for a change, instead of always feeling like we're beneath him.

The upcoming meeting in prison is a key to my trying to move on and refocus my life. I don't know what it will be like, though. I'm running it through my head probably a million and one times a day! I just hope I can sleep the night before.

*Eighteen months after the meeting in prison:*

I got what I wanted from the meeting and then some! Before, what I wanted was to see him broken and sorry for what he did, that he had a good grasp of what he had done. But I wasn't prepared for what this person looked like. I remember him from court: dark hair, glasses, a cocky disposition, a very in-your-face attitude. And now here sits this gray-haired, wrinkled man. He's lost a considerable amount of weight; he's very polite and respectful. Then for a man to bawl and shake and be totally broken—I wanted that, but once I saw it, I didn't know what to do with it.

I was so scared to sit and face this person for whom I'd carried hate, rage, anger, distrust for 10 years. You blame them 110 percent, you despise them, and then you actually sit facing them. Now what do I do? It wasn't until well into the meeting that I was able to get everything out that should have come out right away. And I didn't tell him I forgave him until the very last few minutes. I held off because I thought, "I gotta make sure everything is in place." I've never seen a man bawl like he did. I can't believe you can fake something like that.

Since the meeting, it kind of bothers me that life doesn't seem to hurt like it did. I sit here and think, shouldn't it still be painful? I'm still trying to get this balancing act under control.

I can finally talk about him without fear, even though he's now out of prison. It is really nice not to be afraid of this person! He seems like he's got all his ducks in a row, but he knows if he does one thing, he's back in for a lot more years. I can't expect him to carry this forever, but my theory is that if I can keep him from recommitting anything through my writing to him—which will remind him, "You still have this little ghost in your past"—maybe that will help.

He said, "Once I'm out, am I gonna have to watch my back?" That was kind of interesting, to have him afraid of me for a change. I said, "Nope, I have no intention of doing anything." There's been a balance shift. That gave some power back to me instead of him having all the power, overshadowing everything. He's beneath us now. There's nothing scary about him anymore.

— Sandy Houtz

*Since the meeting,*
*it kind of bothers me that life doesn't seem to hurt like it did.*
*I sit here and think,*
*shouldn't it still be painful?*
*I'm still trying to get this balancing act under control.*

# "I would wake up every morning thinking, 'I hope he dies today.'"

When people ask, "Do you have children?", I don't say I lost my son. I say, "My son was murdered."

In 1985, three months to the day from his college graduation, my son Paul went out to play video games. A young man walked up to him and said, "My mother is dying on the other side of town. Would you give me a ride?" Paul gave him a ride, and he shot Paul and left him to bleed to death in the car by himself. All of those years struggling to pay for braces and teaching him to wash his ears and pick up his room; all those things, then one bullet and it's over.

I was angry. I was angry about Paul's murder; I was angry at the lack of justice. I said, "Give him the death penalty." Of course I ended up shaking hands with Charles, but that was 13 years later.

It was a long journey. My mother died the next year, and my father the next, so I had all three deaths in three years. It kept me busy, but I put off my grief and held onto my anger. Anger can be used in a constructive way, and it kept me here because I thought, "If I commit suicide, who's going to keep the protest letters going?" Every three months I wrote a letter to put in his file. Every six months I made a personal visit to the Board of Pardons and Parole to let them know how much I wanted him kept in prison. I would wake up every morning thinking, "I hope he dies today."

The things my father would do under the guise of religion were just unspeakable. He was a fundamentalist preacher, and he'd drink a glass of ice water and say, "I hate to drink this knowing Paul's burning in hell because you didn't take him to church." He'd say, "That's what you get for sending him to the city to make a business man out of him." He said the reason God killed Paul is because I didn't go to church. Fortunately I had this friend that I could just call and she'd

**THOMAS ANN HINES**

*Last October at the state fair a man walked up covered in tattoos and said, "You spoke in my class in prison." We're standing at the state fair, slinging tears and snot, blowing and carrying on, and he said, "This is my wife, and I'm a hero. You made the difference. Nobody ever told me I could change my life."*

say, "I'll be there." Everybody else kept telling me what to do or feel, but she'd say, "It must be awful to bury your child," rather than saying, "You can't be mad at God."

The way I escaped the hate was that I started asking questions. "Tell me about this guy that killed Paul." I began to get curious about his life. I knew there had to be some factors that influenced who he had become.

The thing that hit like a bolt of lightning was when I was invited by victim services to speak in a prison on a victim impact panel. I was listening to the speakers, watching the prisoners. I was the last speaker, and when I got up to speak, right there was a young, red-headed guy—my Paul frozen in time. He looked at me with what I call hungry eyes—helpless, lonely, filled with pain. I looked at him and thought, "What if that was Paul?"

Rather than give my prepared speech about what scum they were and about how I hoped Charles would rot in hell, I looked at that young man and felt like a mother again. I began to talk to them like they were my boys. When I finished speaking, it was almost like a revival meeting. They were standing up. In the front row, one man, six-feet tall, stood up, tears streaming down his face, and said, "You look just like my mother." What he meant was my compassion and caring. It was a complete turnaround for me. That was not what I went for. It was not the way I had intended things to go. I said, "When can I come back?" That was in 1994, and I'm still going into prisons. The more I go in, the more I want to go in.

I didn't immediately forgive Charles. In fact, I was against starting the victim offender dialogue program. But the more I went into prisons, the more letters I got from prisoners talking about their childhoods. And the more curious I got about Charles.

As I read those letters, I said, "Yeah, the same thing happened to me." I had an uncle who molested me and a father who told me my uncle wouldn't do that because he was a Christian. All my life I've had a whole lot of pain, and hurting people often hurt other people or themselves.

When I was leaving one of the prisons, a guy thanked me for coming. I said, "You are such a nice guy. Why are you here?" He started crying and said, "You know. Every time you talked about Paul, you looked at me." I said, "I don't know what you're talking about." He said, "When I was 17, I killed a guy to steal his car. I was so desperate to get out of town, just like the guy who murdered your son." I said, "I need to talk to Charles."

I talked to friends about meeting with Charles and they said, "No. He's awful, he's a murderer," so I backed out. But I kept having more questions, and I knew he could be out in 1999. I became obsessed with it. I was curious, but my main reason for talking to him was that I wanted to know Paul's last words.

My whole life was focused around a belief system that I had to give up if I was going to see Charles. My daddy put strings on everything. He'd say, "If you love me, go to church and don't wear lipstick." Everybody who did something wrong was going to hell. My religious beliefs were holding me into this little box of an eye for an eye. I had to go totally away from the fundamentalist "Thou shall; thou shalt not." I had to find a spiritual realm that allowed me to be here to learn and to have the free will to make choices. I had to get away from all that rigidity. God's not this big thing on a throne, sitting up there doing bad stuff to people because they are bad.

There had to be room for unconditional love. Charles can never give me back my son. Nothing he can do can fix that. The lesson I learned with Charles came at the end of our meeting. I had the option to put my hand across that table, knowing he couldn't ever give me anything back.

Shaking hands with Charles, putting my hand out, meant that I would accept the hand that held the gun that murdered my son. When I took his hand, I was just going to shake it. But I was overwhelmed. I collapsed on the table with this cry of anguish that took me 13 years to release. I don't believe I ever cried that loud; I was always supposed to cry ladylike. It was a release and a relief.

And he let me see inside his soul. Every time I get a letter from him, every time I write to him, I cry. I'm so connected to him. I'm going to go see him again later this month.

It does not make one bit of sense that Paul Hines was murdered by a guy he tried to help. But when I go into that prison on Thursday, if just one person listens to the message I have to give, then that will be just a little more healing that occurs. It is energizing for me to know I'm in the place that I'm supposed to be. When it's not tiresome, that tells you you're doing the right thing.

— Thomas Ann Hines

# "It was either, I kill myself, or I feel something."

As a young child, I think I was under a lot of smelling, rotting burlap. I was walking around with all that weight and you couldn't really see who I was. As the years have gone by, I have peeled off the burlap, one layer at a time. Finally I'm getting to a point where I'm pretty much standing here on my own two feet. A long time ago it was scary to imagine myself doing that.

When I was six, my parents divorced. I woke up one morning and my father was gone. Then when I was 10, my mother died in a vehicle accident. My older sister, who was 21, became our guardian. A close family friend who lived on the ranch insinuated himself into our lives; Kenny took on a lot of responsibilities and positioned himself as a sort of father as well.

The night after my mother died he started sexually abusing me. He was very dominant, and I didn't really see any way around it. He worked hard at separating me from my family and, because of my shame, I ended up working with him to cover it up. I got good at lying and manipulation. In one sense, I was the kid that got away with everything; in another sense, I was the kid that slipped between the cracks.

At 14 I began to push away. Then, at my sister's wedding when I was 16, I just grabbed him and went, "No. Get the fuck away from me." Right then, it was like I got a little bit of power back. But nobody knew until I was 21 when I pressed charges.

I think I projected a glittering image during those years, but I really blamed myself and had very low self-esteem. I lost a lot of dignity and self-respect. I had cut off my emotions so much that I couldn't feel pain anymore. I used to walk up to a brick wall, hit it hard, and not feel the pain. One time I walked up to a windshield and went wham. It really freaked me out that it didn't hurt. I was hanging backwards off of balconies on the 25th floor going, "Wow, this is

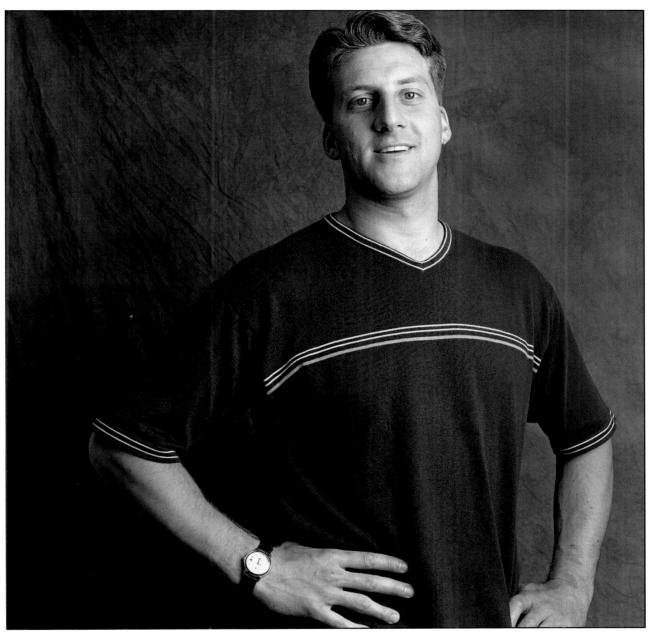

BION DOLMAN

*Meeting with Kenny was my first step from being a victim towards being a* survivor. *Now I want to go beyond being a survivor and integrate what happened into my entire experience. There's no way I can ever outlive it or outrun it. I tried that for years, and it just doesn't work that way. I think the only way to deal with it is to transcend it.*

great," driving a motorcycle or car down a freeway at 220 km an hour. It was either I kill myself, or I feel something. One of the two. I was so shut down, but really I'm an emotional person and I couldn't handle not feeling.

I've beaten myself up a lot about those years. "Oh, if you were stronger, you wouldn't have put up with that shit." I was a loser because I wasn't strong enough to get out of it. It was easy to be a victim and say, "Oh, I had no choice." But that does damage.

I knew that behind me there was nothing, nowhere to go. Even if I felt like telling, say my sister, the shame I felt was too much. So I made that decision. I stepped through that doorway and that's what changed my life. I have to accept that. But it's still really hard to look back and respect a 10-year-old's decision to submit to that man. It's hard for me as an adult to have confidence in that little boy and to say, "Okay, for whatever reason, you made that decision," without feeling I was weak because I didn't kick and scream.

I had pretty much written off those years as a waste of time. Now I've been going to see a therapist, and we've done a lot of work at putting value on those years. I realize I learned a lot. I've learned to read people, to understand people's motives. I really pick up when somebody's trying to manipulate me and when they're lying. I've worked hard at setting up boundaries with people. I'm listening more and more to that voice in my head that says, "I don't want to do this. It doesn't feel right." I'm learning to trust and follow that inner voice. I've slowly gotten a sense of accomplishment and self-worth out of all this.

I know things that a 50- or 70-year-old man doesn't know. In that way the experience has been a blessing of sorts.

I eventually pressed charges at the age of 21. One reason I did was because there are two young boys who live right by him. I could not handle the thought of him sexually abusing them and me not doing anything about it. It was the flip side of the coin. One side of the coin was me wanting to punish him; the flip side was making sure that he was exposed and couldn't harm anybody else. I could not have forgiven myself if years later someone said, "Oh, did you know Kenny was abusing the boys next door?" and I'd raise my hand, "Oh, he abused me too . . ."

The charges were pressed in the name of the Queen, her Crown and dignity, and I was just a witness. I didn't like that bullshit—this happened to me. It didn't happen to the fucking Queen! I was always a bit pissed off about that.

I don't want a vengeful or punitive justice system. I want a system that equally represents the victim and the one prosecuted. It's ridiculous the amount of special attention that a defendant gets. Everything was fed to him. All he had to do was be willing to participate, and that was all done on the taxpayer's dime. Meanwhile, I've had to struggle to get my life back on track. I've paid for my therapy although it was partly reimbursed through criminal compensation. I've had to make the sacrifice and effort.

If somebody commits a crime, this system gives them a special status. I don't agree with that. If you hurt another person, you have to be made accountable for that, and I don't think sitting in a cell is what is going to do it. It would be better for perpetrators to sit down with their victims and talk to them and understand what they have gone through. They should have to take that on. If the victim were able to say, "I'm a person. This is who I am and what I felt. This is what you've done to my life," I think that would have a greater effect.

I reached a point in my therapy where I needed to confront Kenny. Visualizing saying all these things to him is not the same as sitting down with the actual person and saying what you've wanted to. So I met him. For the most part it was about me taking power back. I was taking the garbage that was in my system and saying, "Here, I don't want it anymore." There was a part of me that wanted him to feel guilty and ashamed, to feel all those emotions that he made me feel. But for the most part it was me cleansing myself, saying, "I don't need this anymore. I'm not carrying it. It's yours. If you don't want to pick it up, that's fine, but it's not mine anymore."

I had a lot of really good feelings immediately after the meeting, but it took longer for things to really settle in. For me it was the first step down the road to saying, "I'm tired of being a victim."

In a lot of ways I've been able to take the experience and build on it. I've been able to transcend the experience. For a lot of years I was on the other side of the fence. I was happy in that spot because I had something to blame everything on. If it wasn't Kenny, it was my father. If it wasn't my father, it was my mother. It's a pretty gray and shitty place to be in.

After the meeting with Kenny I think I forgave him. I've never read the Bible, but I thought that forgiveness in the biblical sense meant giving up too much of yourself and letting the offender off the hook without really being able to express what happened to you. But I don't think it's about that.

I was able to forgive Kenny because I was able to express what had happened to me. I reclaimed part of myself in order to forgive Kenny. I take this part of myself back from you and I forgive you because I'm whole. That's what it meant to me.

Afterward, when he walked up to me and wanted to say good-bye, I was really surprised that I shook his hand and said, "I wish you the best, Kenny." I was surprised that I was able to do that. In that moment, I meant it. I didn't want him to suffer eternally. I think that's transcending!

Now I want to meet him again. I've changed a lot. I've got more questions.

When one of the facilitators and I went for lunch during the meeting, he looked at me and said, "You know, you might want to let him speak sometime." I just kept reloading the shotgun and letting him have it with both barrels. Now I want to know about it from his side, to hear what his perspective was.

Being a victim will make you hard because you keep the hate and anger and shame and guilt. And it will make you soft because there are people who will see you only as a victim and coddle you because of that. You'll become soft, too, because you will never challenge yourself and never move past that experience.

Once you move past that and become a survivor, you've got to keep moving. There comes a time in life when you have to move on.

— Bion Dolman

*"It's like a jigsaw puzzle
where there's more than one way
to put the pieces together."*

# "I thought, 'I'm going to run until I'm not angry anymore.'"

There are actually two stories. The first one starts with my father's death. I was 12, and I felt responsible for his death because I figured, if I hadn't called and distracted my mother at the hospital at the moment I did, maybe she would have gotten his fever down. Also, my mom had said, "Why don't you write your father a note?" I didn't because I didn't realize his illness was serious.

Then, when I was 13, my brother's friend raped me. In my mind, this was my punishment for killing my father. After that a lot of inappropriate anger came out. Little things would set me off. I became real inner-punitive and used to cut myself. I also tried to make myself as plain as possible. He said, "You've got beautiful eyes," so I pulled out all my eyebrows and eyelashes. I never told anyone. I felt, "If you don't deal with this, it will go away."

When my second assailant grabbed me, my first thought was, "My God, I'm reporting it this time." I realized then that these experiences don't go away—they just fester—and I wasn't carrying this hidden secret. The second assault was a real wake-up call.

It happened in 1985 when I was 36 years old. My husband, daughter, and I went to the state park, which we often did, and I went for a jog on the beach. A man came running and grabbed me, took me into a wooded area, and sexually assaulted me. He beat me pretty bad, especially around the head, and broke my nose.

The night I came home from the hospital I got a threatening phone call. He said something obscene and then, "I want you." The next morning I went out for a walk. At that point I had a "screw you" attitude toward my offender. Running is an integral part of my life. "You think, because of what you did to me, I'm not going to continue? You're really wrong!"

I went through a period where I constantly ruminated. It's like I had a continuous-play videotape going on in my head and I couldn't

PENNY BEERNTSEN

*You have to reconfigure your life. It's like a jigsaw puzzle. I used to think there was one way that things fit together. When they didn't fit that way, the world was out of alignment. But now when a piece doesn't fit well here, it feels important to me that it might fit somewhere else. The key is trying to find where that piece of the puzzle fits.*

149

turn it off. And I needed to turn it off. What worked was while I was in the shower, I'd say, "Okay, you can have a pity party in here by yourself; you can feel sorry for yourself. As long as you are in the shower, you can think about what happened. You've got a half hour to do that." I don't know if that's healthy or not, but it worked for me.

A lot of what helped me to heal were supportive family and friends. I remember one morning, at a real low point, I opened the door to get the morning newspaper and between the doors was a little card with a quote from Hemingway's *Farewell to Arms:* "The world breaks everyone; then some become strong at the broken places." And my husband was a huge part of my recovery. A less patient man would have left.

Since I was a witness I couldn't be in the courtroom after I testified the first day, so I was

wild. I would put on my running shoes; one day I ran probably 20 miles. I thought, "I'm going to run until I'm not angry anymore." Generally my legs gave out before my anger. When the assailant was found guilty, my daughter said, "Oh, now this is finally over!" But I knew it had just started.

I said to my therapist, "If they find him not guilty, that's it for me. I'm gonna kill myself." She said, "You were his victim, for an hour on the beach. Now it's your choice whether to remain in the victim role, or whether you want to use the experience to be stronger." I wanted to kick her in the teeth, but she was right.

I wrote a suicide note. I was going to walk out into Lake Michigan and swim till hypothermia took me. I took the suicide note and jogged from our house to the beach; the round trip was probably 14 miles. I went to the scene by myself, I stood right under the trees where he assaulted me, and I just tore that note up. It was a real healing thing. I remember feeling, "That's it, Steve. It's over. You don't have any more control."

I was grateful when he was found guilty because I thought he should be held accountable, but I had a real sadness, too. I wondered "What went wrong? Why didn't someone pick up on his difficulties?" I knew that his family's life had been changed forever by this.

At one point I told my therapist that it was a burden to have to testify because he was so young and the consequences could be so great. She said, "You should want to kill the son of a bitch!" That may have been okay for her, but it really shut down the line of communication for me. I thought, "Okay, I guess I don't discuss this with her."

Not quite two years after the assault, I heard a speaker talk about restorative justice. I remember feeling, "Wow, for the first time someone understands how I feel towards the offender." Not that I wasn't angry with him and didn't think he should be accountable, but I was concerned about what would happen to him. If he comes out of prison no better than he went in, we've done a great disservice to society. The speaker also talked about letting go of anger and trying to rebuild. I felt euphoric, as though a huge weight had been lifted. It was what I'd been trying to talk about with my therapist, but she wasn't hearing it, and my family wasn't hearing it.

I thought about victim-offender mediation in my case, but because my offender maintains his innocence, I was advised that it would be counterproductive. I did go through training to become a mediator. I hoped that maybe I could stop some other kid who gets in trouble by helping him to understand the impact his action had on the people he victimized.

When I first started speaking in prison, I was addressing sex offender treatment groups. I wanted to help them recognize the connection between their behavior and what their victims experienced. Little did I realize how much I was going to take from the process! I was surprised that these men started opening up about their own victimization. A lot of them have a real sense of shame. And they said, not "Poor me," but, "I connect with you because I've been there; then I turned around and victimized someone else."

After my first assault, I babysat for a little neighbor boy. Because he was a boy, I wanted to hurt him. I didn't, but the impulse was there. So for me it's real easy to see where these offenders are coming from. I think we're all capable of murder and mercy. It's only by the grace of God that some of us are able to take the healing path that we do.

Hearing these prisoners' stories, I wonder how they even survived. Horrible, horrible stories, dysfunctional families, no support. How can you undo that damage? We need to rethink what goes on inside prisons because of what happens to people when they're there. I believe the ultimate apology is not to re-offend.

My work with victims and offenders is where I sense I'm meant to be. For the first time in my life, I know who I am. It's not tied to my being a wife, mother, or whatever, but it is something internal. If someone had told me in 1985 that part of my healing—an essential part of my healing—was going to take place inside the walls of a maximum security prison, I'd have said, "Are you nuts?!"

If God asked, "Would you like me to take this experience away from you?" I've often wondered what my response would be. Initially I'd have said, "Of course, why are you even asking that question?" But now I think I would say, "Definitely not!" just because of where it's taken me.

I need to put a caveat on that. I don't mean, "Gee, it would be a wonderful thing if other women were assaulted because they might find out who they really are!" But I do think, whether it's being a victim of crime or suffering a great loss, such an experience becomes an integral part of who we are.

My faith was deeply strengthened, even though there were times I didn't feel anything. The Maundy Thursday, Good Friday, and Easter sunrise services became real important to me. It's a reminder not only that Christ died for us, but that he is present with us now in all circumstances. As the years go on and I hear more offender stories and more victim stories, I have a growing sense that we're all sinners and we all fall short and we're in this journey together. In between we take divergent paths.

In some ways the word *recovery* is appropriate. I had to go back, because I hadn't dealt with stuff earlier. I don't think you ever get over such an experience. You get through it, but you keep growing as you hear other people's stories and learn how other people have dealt with similar things.

I had an interesting dream that I was back on the beach where I had been assaulted, and someone had built a fire. There was a rabbit on the fire, and the rabbit's underside was being singed, but the rabbit was still alive. In my dream, I rescue the rabbit. I take it off the fire, and I take it home and nurture it back to health. My therapist viewed me as the rabbit. Maybe the underlying theme of the dream was that I could save myself or that I could get through this. Or perhaps there were others who would help me and nurture me and bring me back.

I think of myself like the Velveteen Rabbit. The book talks about how you're not real until you get all the fur rubbed off. A lot of my fur's rubbed off and I am real. I have a sense of self now.

My experience has been like an S-chain where the links don't go all the way around but hook on to one another. At first I thought it was serendipity, all these different events happening. Now they all seem to be connected; it seems like Providence. There's a curve, and you can't see what's at the end of that link. And there are obstacles along the way. Then you get to the end, and, wow, there's another link there. And you keep going. The links are open; there's good around the bend.

— Penny Beerntsen

*After my first assault,*
*I babysat for a little neighbor boy.*
*Because he was a boy, I wanted to hurt him.*
*I didn't, but the impulse was there.*
*It's only by the grace of God*
*that some of us are able to take the healing path that we do.*

# "The real Sandy was full of shame and hate and fear of rejection."

When I was a young girl, my father died and my elder brother came to live with us. I call him Satan himself. He would beat me tremendously, lock me up, do incest to me. I was looking for a way out and one day I met this guy who I thought would be my knight in shining armor. We dated about a year and he married me.

Ultimately this guy was really a second-level devil in my home. He was very violent, so I decided to move out. He started watching me. On Labor Day weekend, 1974, he called me and said, "You'll be dead Friday." Then he came to my home, choked me unconscious, and put a shotgun between my eyes at close range. It blew out one side of my face. It's a miracle I still have a head, let alone eyes or ears. God gave me a chance to be a testimony to his mercy and glory.

At first I was in a big void with darkness all around me. But I wanted some light. That's when I started to decide that it didn't matter what I looked like on the outside; I had to get clean and feel whole on the inside.

Every time I went to sleep, I dreamed about the shooting, about the whole scene. One day there in the hospital I began to pray, "If you're real, if you are that big a God, will you take these nightmares away from me?" I remember almost feeling the presence of God, a peace, and the dreams left immediately. I said, "Something's happening here," and I began to read the Bible. I began to realize God's miracle was in motion, so I started to try to act it out.

Norman Vincent Peale's book, *The Power of Positive Thinking*, opened my eyes. I started looking inside of me and facing the truth—the shame of knowing that even though he tried to kill me, I was still in love with the man; the fear of knowing that though she looked big and strong, the real Sandy was weeping inside and was full of shame and hate and fear of rejection. That book opened my eyes about the power of

SANDRA (SANDY)MURPHY

*A lot of activists hate the word "victim," but the truth is that we are. And the truth is that we've survived. I want to use both terms: I am a victim and I am a triumphant survivor. At first I was really a zombie, a walking dead woman. Now I'm alive.*

positive thinking. No matter what the negative, you look within yourself to see your strength. I started to understand, but it didn't happen overnight.

Suicide visited me—I tried it while in the hospital. But what gave me the drive to live was when my kids came to visit me. My mother was not what they needed; I wanted to be back home to make it right for my children.

The doctors wouldn't allow me to see my face. They would say, "It's going to be fine." That was a lie. The truth is important to me. The truth helped me to be able to stand and say, "This is ugly, but you can do it."

It is so important to tell the truth. That's what the book I wrote is about—getting the cleansing through the truth. I'm telling my story through my eyes; this is a truth that happened to Sandy and I don't care who doesn't like it. That book cannot be still![1]

There were a lot of tears in writing it, and it took me four years because of so much pain. I started to understand that the nightmare of it all was the little girl who was unwanted, a black sheep, a motherless child. It was about my mother, and I began to get cleansing from my mother. I'd been taught lies and told not to tell or live the truth. In this book I told everything. Writing that book cleansed me and made me feel whole. It was like a butterfly, like my soul released. I can't even describe the energy that said, "Now that chapter is over."

I forgave my ex-husband, but that did not happen overnight. He did 10 years in prison and now is living here in this city somewhere. I had visions of his murder for years, but, as I grew to love the Lord, I knew I wasn't going to be able to get a breakthrough until I forgave him.

Forgiveness to me means to process pain. As long as you're hurting, you can't even have a stepping-stone to forgiveness. I wanted his physical body to hurt, and that was destroying my mind. When I forgave him, I was free. Now I could pray for his soul, for his spirit to get new so he would stop hurting people. But forgiveness doesn't let the person off the hook. They will pay, but it's not your responsibility to inflict that or see them suffer.

I try to use my own life to heal others, because people can't heal from someone who's never been in any pain. I have a radio talk show, and I do Christian family therapy. A part of my ministry is called "Inside Out"; I go inside prisons and do healing. But as I'm ministering to others, I'm ministering to myself.

— Sandra (Sandy) Murphy

[1] Sandy's book, *Too Bad It Wasn't a Dream,* is available from Fair Care Center, 3116 Telge, Suite D, Houston, TX 77054.

*The doctors wouldn't allow me to see my face.*

*They would say, "It's going to be fine."*

*That was a lie.*

*The truth is important to me.*

*The truth helped me to be able to stand and say,*

*"This is ugly, but you can do it."*

# "My life is different in so many ways."

Two boys came to the house I was visiting. They had two guns and told me to go in the living room and lie down. They discussed among themselves who was going to kill me and by which gun. Then they pulled the trigger. It was at point-blank range. I remember it explicitly. I will remember it until I die.

The doctors gave me a two percent chance of survival. It took me about a year to learn everything from scratch—how to sit, how to walk, how to swallow, how to talk. Those boys took my vision, and they also took the right side of me. I still have trouble talking and walking. But I don't allow myself a great deal of time to mourn.

I lived 45 years the way I wanted to. I had a full life, a very good life, made up of me and my sons. But then Jackie Millar died. I invited some of my best friends and we had a burial of Jackie Millar. Now my life is different in so many ways.

I live it mainly for youth. I talk to youth in schools, in jails, in prisons. I've been going to prison two or three times a week and I love it! And I speak to justice and community people, too.

You'll think I'm strange, but I believe the good Lord said to me, "I wonder if you'll do this small thing for me." He wanted me to talk to young people, to point them in the right direction. I believe everything happens for a purpose.

People think I'm looney, but it is easier for me to forgive than not to. I'm like a mother to all these kids, and one thing mothers do is forgive. I forgive Craig and Josh for what they've done. It was rather easy. I believe that they made an error—granted, a great error!—but an error. But forget? Never!

Toward Craig, the one who shot me in the head, I feel like a mother. I met with him and we must have talked three hours. I wanted him to see what he had done to me. I wanted to see him

JACQUELINE M. MILLAR

*I died on November 4, 1995. I died, and then I got resurrected. The Lord said, "Maybe you can stop one youth if you tell your story."*

159

in person, and I wanted to hear him apologize. I didn't ask for an apology, but I hoped he would give me one. He did, and I accepted. And then I asked permission to hug him. I don't think he's received a lot of hugs. I hugged him like a mother hugs her son, and then I went home. Seeing him in person sitting across from me, hearing him say, "I'm sorry, I'm sorry," was so important! If I hadn't met him, it would have been harder to go on with my life.

With Joshua it's different. I don't know yet. I only met him at his second trial. He apologized to me at his sentencing, although I'm not so sure of his sincerity. I haven't gone to see him yet, but I probably will.

As for the justice system—the policemen and the district attorneys were wonderful, but they need to be quiet for once and listen to us. They say "Shhhh" to the victim, but to the perpetrator, it's "Whatever you want to say." That doesn't seem fair. We're not dumb bunnies; we have good ideas. They need to be quiet and listen to the victim!

— Jacqueline M. Millar

*You'll think I'm strange,*
*but I believe the good Lord said to me,*
*"I wonder if you'll do this small thing for me."*
*He wanted me to talk to young people,*
*to point them in the right direction.*

# "I could see my hands going around his throat, killing him . . ."

An experience like this causes you to go deep into your deepest soul, your deepest gut feelings, and lets your deepest core come out. If you don't, transcendence doesn't happen.

In 1993, two 19-year-old strangers broke into my sister's apartment and murdered her for her car and 13 dollars. Each was given the death penalty. The man subsequently died in prison of AIDS and the woman is still on death row.

My sister and I bonded at a very young age. I had always looked after her, so it really impacted me when she was tortured and killed. I became dysfunctional and just fell apart. I wasn't sleeping, I didn't eat well, I couldn't focus, I couldn't work. I went into a serious clinical depression. I had experienced a depression in '84, but it was not of this scope. This was my first traumatic experience where I realized I was not in control.

A big moment came in January of '94 when I wrote a letter to another person as a kind of witness and said, "I am surrendering my will to God." I basically surrendered control, surrendered my pride, and that started me on a spiritual journey. The next step came about two years later in a Bible study when I recognized God's abundant love. I have two sons, and I knew how much I loved them, but I knew that God's love was greater than that! I started concentrating on receiving God's love.

I was raised Catholic and have gone to church all my life. But realizing God's love was a defining moment. That brought me up a notch, and then I went through a period of acceptance—accepting what had happened in my life, including the murder.

When the guy went on trial 11 months after the murder, I was in a rage. I saw him in the courtroom and starting walking towards him. It was like I was in some sort of zone. I could see my hands going around his throat, killing him. I got within 20 feet of him and my inner voice

162

JOHN SAGE

*For me the key was letting go, just trying to give up control in my life—or thinking I had control—and seeking God's will for my life. That started me on a spiritual journey that led me to a better place.*

said, "Stop. You've got a wife and two kids. Stop!" I don't know that I would have gone through with it, but I was in enough of a rage that I *could* have killed him.

About four years after my surrender to God, I realized I had forgiven these people. The female offender was scheduled to be executed and "20/20," the television show, called. "Aren't you excited about this execution?" they asked. I said, "No," and when I hung up, I realized that in the conversation I was trying to get mad and couldn't. I felt this great freedom—I'm not mad, I'm not enraged!

This forgiveness was a result of a closer walk with God, a grace that came as a result of my spiritual journey. It was almost the last step. I know a lot of people forgive earlier, but I think if you forgive too quickly, that can create problems.

The next step was taking this experience and using it to help others. I got invited into a project which involves victims coming into prison and meeting with offenders—not the offenders that offended them, but similar offenders. I'd never seen a group of people with less empathy in my life, but I saw things happen. People's lives changed over a period of 90 days. I saw men admit to things they had never admitted to anybody.

Now I coordinate a victim-offender encounter project like this, and I also do reentry classes at prison.[1] I like working with victims. I like working with prisoners. I like the spiritual side of this work. It's my ministry. If you had told me after the murder that I'd be doing this, I'd have said, "You're crazy. That's the last thing I would do!"

— John Sage

[1] Bridges To Life invites victims of violent crime into prison to interact during a 12-week program with inmate volunteers who are soon to be released.

Bridges To Life is located at 12727 Kimberley Lane, Suite 303. Houston, TX 77024. Telephone: 713/463-7200.

*An experience like this*
*causes you to go deep into your deepest soul,*
*your deepest gut feelings,*
*and lets your deepest core come out.*
*If you don't,*
*transcendence doesn't happen.*

# "I was angry and came in contact with many angry people."

In 1985 I was assaulted by my ex-boyfriend. He broke my neck and I was paralyzed. I prayed, I leaned on my faith in God, and I started gaining back some of the feelings in my body. That's a blessing. But I've been in a wheelchair for the last 15 years.

I formed the first organization here in Houston dedicated to all victims of violent crime, and I chaired it from '89 to '94.

We didn't have an organization here that addressed issues pertaining to people like me. It is important for us to have a say in the parole process. It was important to me to be able to say that I don't think our offenders ought to be out on furlough. I thought it was terrible; I didn't get any furlough! The person who victimized me got out on furlough after a parole denial, and I wouldn't have known anything about it had he not started contacting my friends. I wanted to make sure I had the freedom to move around in my own city without having to worry about whether he is going to be standing at my front door. Now we have been given the opportunity to be able to make free long-distance calls, any time of the day or night, and to find out exactly where our perpetrators are.

I didn't go through the "whys," and I don't think I was ever angry with God. Things happen; that's just what life is about. I never went through the "crys" either. I can't explain it, but I never felt sorry for myself. I've learned not to dwell on what or why it happened. I guess in a sense I have forgiven, because I've left that behind me. Forgiveness is not to say it's all right that it happened, but it's a process of getting out of that spot and moving on.

Since I've been in this wheelchair, I've met many wonderful people. And I've been able to help many people. We're here to serve each other; that's what gives life meaning.

— Patricia Roberts-Gates

PATRICIA ROBERTS-GATES

*When I was in the hospital—I don't know if it was an illusion or what—I seemed to be ascending up into the sky. When I got up so far, a voice told me I couldn't go any farther because I hadn't bought any real estate! I guess I came back a different person. It wasn't my time. I had other things to do.*

# "You have all these little numbers, but none of them work."

Overall, it's pretty simple: everything in your life changes! Everything is turned upside down. From the time you get up in the morning until you go to bed at night, nothing is ever the same again. Your life becomes divided into two parts—B.C. and A.C.—before the crime and after the crime. And you're angry. You want life as it was before. That's when you think, "God, I wish I could just wake up."

In 1986 I was 43 and lived in a beautiful home overlooking the city of Austin. I felt secure and safe. It was Labor Day weekend. My daughter had just moved out to go to college and my son had spent the night somewhere else. I got up in the morning and went to take a shower. As I was walking from the shower to get my robe, I spotted a man dressed in a Ninja suit. He had these funny little boots and gloves and a turban. Everything was covered but his eyes. In his hand, raised over his head, was a big knife.

My first instinct was that it was a joke. Then I knew that it wasn't a joke and it wasn't a dream, and I was in deep shit trouble.

He knocked me down, tied up my hands and feet, blindfolded me, and during the next hour and a half raped and stabbed me. I could feel him pacing the room and he talked a lot. He was full of an incredible amount of anger. He stabbed me in the chest and in the neck and hammered a knife into my skull. Then he beat me in the head with a hammer and left me for dead. The plastic surgeon who put my head back together said there were eight to 10 areas of impact and hundreds of stitches.

It was all horrible to deal with, but the rape was maybe the worst because of the humiliation. I felt ripped inside out in every way—physically, emotionally, spiritually, sexually. I felt like I was unlovable, untouchable, a kind of throw-away person.

Being a crime victim is very humiliating because you feel slimy. There is always some

ELLEN HALBERT

*I'm real proud of the job that I did in my healing journey—I did a damn good job of healing. I like to talk about it because I'm so proud of it, and I'm always thinking that maybe somebody else can catch it. But I'm also careful because I can't expect everyone to heal the same way I did.*

169

self-blame; we can always find millions of ways we may have brought this on ourselves. I wondered if I had set myself up as a victim. But I was in my own bathroom. I can't say I was in the wrong place at the wrong time. You feel that you should have been able to control the situation.

Then there is the matter of your sexuality, the most private part of you. I know that the attack was nothing about sex. Having me tied up, having me hop everywhere, screaming at me, was about power. But to have that most special part of you, that you share with someone you love, be taken is a very degrading, humiliating thing. When I would go places, I felt like everybody was pointing at me, that I had this big red "R"—Rape victim—tattooed on my forehead. I had to pull on all my strength to heal from that, and eventually I was transformed. Now I can talk about it and about how, by God, I survived and am stronger than I ever was before. It's a process. You turn shame into pride.

If you are vindicated that what happened to you is absolutely not your fault, you don't need to bear nearly so much shame. This means getting a lot of information so that victims may come to some kind of resolution that vindicates them. That was the most frustrating thing for me—I got none. I still resent that.

I remember in the hospital being so angry with God and wondering what of the million things I had done I was being punished for. I felt I must deserve what had happened to me, even though I had always felt like a child of God and loved by God. But it didn't take me very long to realize that it wasn't God punishing me. I ended

up going full circle, realizing that since I had survived, I had gotten strength from somewhere. Instead of questioning God, I began thanking God for giving me the strength from somewhere. Instead of questioning God, I began thanking God for giving me the strength to survive. I believed that my faith was going to be strengthened in the healing.

Luckily, I think I understood that my survival depended on my not being eaten up inside with anger. Rage was going to destroy me up if I didn't forgive this man. I'm a big believer in forgiveness, but I don't believe that I have to go somewhere and say, "I forgive you." It wasn't that I said those words; it was just the way I felt about it. It's something that you need for yourself.

I'm not going to say that my healing was through another person because it wasn't, but I met a wonderful man who loved to listen to me and made me feel very special. I don't know how people survive violent crime without family who loves them. I got a lot of help through group, too. After a couple of months, I said to my counselor, "I think I'm crazy. I'm losing my mind." She said, "I think it's time for support group." It was a wonderful place to be. I told them I was there because I thought I was losing my mind. They said, "Oh, we've all been there."

A year or two after the assault, I was invited during Crime Victims' Week to give a speech on the steps of the capitol. I thought there would be a little group and I would make a few remarks. When I got there, there were TV cameras and chairs all over the place. Everybody was there, and I was the keynote speaker! I almost left because I was absolutely terrified, but it was one of the single most empowering events that happened to me. The audience was so interested in what I had to say that I was just bowled over. So I began looking for opportunities to be heard.

In 1991 I got so noisy that I caught the attention of Governor Ann Richards. She appointed me as the first crime victim to be on the Texas Board of Criminal Justice. I began touring prisons and became totally frustrated with what I saw. I couldn't believe what we were doing— this tiny space for two was supposed to heal somebody? I began looking for something else. Then I started hearing about restorative justice, and that was the answer for me.

I want to make all kinds of changes. I want better things for victims. That's happening, and I have a passion for that. But the thing I'm not seeing happen is on the other side, on the offender's side. I want the prison system to change for the better; I'm so frustrated about the way we do our punishment.

Justice for me would be something so bizarre that it would never happen in our punitive system. The offender would go to prison, and while there, people would reach out to work with him on his anger and rage toward women. I'd love to have people try to figure out if there was something in this man's soul that could be saved. Maybe there isn't, but you'd have to prove to me that there isn't. In almost every one of God's creatures there is a spark of goodness, and if we give it enough of the right kind of fuel, it will grow.

The man who did this to me was captured, and we had a trial right before he turned 19. He was sentenced to life in prison, which in Texas is about 20 years. I often wonder about him. He was full of an incredible amount of anger. Since he's been in prison, he's been in lockdown most of the time because he's real assaultive. Is he assaultive because he's half-black and half-white? Or because he's frightened? Or is he really just a rotten human being? I used to think I met the devil in my bathroom, but I don't know. Maybe he was just a product of his environment. I have a lot of questions about the man who did this to me.

At a conference I heard a woman speak, along with the drunk driver who killed her sister. They had had a mediation and came to talk about it. I remember being jealous in a way that they had been able to come to a place of healing, to have all these questions answered, to get to know the other's life. I remember leaving there and walking the streets and thinking about it. I wanted that. I wanted to be able to ask those questions. I asked the victim-offender mediation program, and they talked to the offender. He refused. He wasn't willing because he'd have to admit his guilt in order to participate. But I still hope one day to find out what he was like as a baby. I'm convinced he wasn't born to rape and murder. I'm curious; I've always had this driving need to know where society failed him.

Someone described this journey we go through as trying to open a safe. You have all these little numbers in your pocket and you pull them out, but none of them work. It's because that's the old way of getting through life. Now there's a new way, but you don't really know what it is. You have to come up with a new order. I rebuilt my life into some other kind of life. I am thrilled to be alive, and I'm absolutely so happy with my life that it's almost scary! I keep wanting to use a better word than *blessing*, but that's the way I feel.

Life is really an inspiring journey for me these days. I've learned about myself—and others around me—that people have an incredible capacity to heal from even the most incredible trauma. It's pretty wonderful. I wouldn't ever want to go through this again. But I feel truly blessed for the opportunities I've had because of the horrible, terrible thing that happened in my bathroom.

— Ellen Halbert

*If you are vindicated that what happened to you is absolutely not your fault,*

*you don't need to bear nearly so much shame.*

*This means getting a lot of information.*

*That was the most frustrating thing for me—*

*I got none.*

*I still resent that.*

# "It was my fault and I'm no good. I've been tainted."

I've got a picture in my mind of a rose. It's blue, a single bud. I watch it blossoming. And it's blue because it's different, in some way unique. It's a metaphor that works for me about healing and growing.

Not that my story is so unique, because lots of people have been through such things. You know the stories; eventually, they're all the same. Evil is quite banal and unimaginative.

I was abused physically by my father and sexually abused by several uncles, brothers, and my father. Any kind of abuse you can imagine went on—anywhere from fondling to very violent assault and rape.

I'm also a victim of ritual abuse. A lot of it was done outside around fires, and I can see creatures coming out of the fire. I know that some of the things I remember are not real. They're either demonic, or the way my mind created monsters to answer for what was done to me. I

don't know that it matters which it was. What matters is that it was traumatic and it hurt me.

Some incidents stand out. One was a particularly violent assault by my father when he raped me. I felt like something in me died that day, and I made an agreement with life: I won't ever trust anybody or love anybody. That night I became pregnant. I was 15 years old. I miscarried at about five months. No one knew I was pregnant, and no one knew I miscarried. That was, I think, one of my most intense points of needing to look at the issue of forgiving myself. I thought if I had told somebody, if I had taken better care of myself, the baby might not have died. When I recently told David, my counselor, about it, he took me out in his boat, and we had a memorial for her, just he and I. It was an incredible experience. It was validating. That child's life had meaning.

A lot of the things I carried are the typical abuse factors: that it was my fault and I'm no

GAYLE MACNAB

*I woke up one morning, years ago, with a thought in my head, just as clear as if I heard it out loud: "They had half of my life; I'll be damned if I'll give 'em the rest." One of my favorite scriptures is in Psalm 84 where it says, "I've set my heart on pilgrimage." I set my heart on this journey at that point, although there are still times when I get lost again.*

good. I've been tainted. I made several suicide attempts as a teenager. Self-worth was a huge issue. I had been told so many times that I couldn't ever be good for anything. All the different threats and lies twist your mind. In a strange turnabout I am now, as a counselor, telling people all the things that I needed to hear for so long.

I remember very clearly creating boxes in my head, and I put the stuff that happened to me in those boxes and shut their lids. For years I had a completely other fantasy world. When things got rough here, I went over to that world and hid in those boxes with no outside handles. It was a very distinct world. I was a different person with different names; everything was different. It was of my own making. But it got to the point where I couldn't make choices about whether to be here or there. Both worlds became destructive. They both became crazy, and I wasn't sure where I was anymore. Then came a very dramatic point in my healing.

I became a Christian, and while praying, I felt that those boxes were not a good place to go. I felt I had, at that moment, the power to make the decision not to go there anymore, and if I made the decision, then I could be free from that. I remember literally arguing with God, saying, "But that means I have to stay here all the time." I made the choice to stay in the real world, but I remember being really angry at God for that. I was about 16 or 17.

I've decided that what happened to me can become my gift or my albatross, and I'm the only one that can choose. I'll never be thankful for

what happened, and I wouldn't choose this route again. But I'm thankful for what I've learned from it, for the gifts it has given me, the insights, the compassion. And I've had some real surprises along the way. One of the biggest was the change in my heart towards offenders. When I turned the corner into having hope and concern for the offender's side, a number of things just released for me. That first meeting I had with offenders, when I walked into the room and saw these people and realized that I didn't hate them—that day will be etched in my mind forever.

When I learned that my counselor, David, also worked with offenders, I said, "How can you work with people like that?" Eventually, though, I went to prison with him, and I was terrified. A lot of things went through my mind. I had my Christian beliefs about the work God has done in me and about forgiveness, yet I thought, "I hate what these people do. I hate *them*, too." I wanted them to have warts and horns. Then I walked into the room and saw a group of men who could have been having a business meeting. The more I heard from them, the more I hurt for them, the more I felt their pain.

They all told me what they were in for and what their sentences were. I told them what it was like to be victimized and what legacy I was left with, that it doesn't all go away, even though there's been lots of healing for me. I said, "What you need to know is what it does to the person's soul and spirit." I remember thinking, "Is this vengeance? Am I getting back at them by telling them how awful it is?" And I thought, "I don't think so." I wanted them to hear it. I wanted them to know how hard it is and what it does.

At the end of the meeting I talked about this battle within me. "I wanted to hate all of you and I can't do it. I didn't want to feel compassion for you." And then one of the guys spoke up and said, "I don't want you to like me. I want you to hate me." And I said, "I can't do that for you." They wanted me to yell and scream at them, and I couldn't do that. I tried to explain to them how that wouldn't heal me and that there wouldn't be healing in it for them. It wasn't what I wanted to do.

I couldn't imagine that what I did at the prison could be helpful to the men there. It hadn't occurred to me that it would be important for them; this was about me. But I began to understand that it was about much more than me. That was astounding.

I have different feelings toward my actual offenders. Much of that is because they have never acknowledged nor confessed anything. That's not something I can ever fix. But as long as I believed they couldn't change, I was still angry, and that took a lot of energy, a lot of focus. Now I don't have to do that anymore.

I call this forgiveness, or at least part of forgiveness. When I talk about forgiveness, I talk about what it isn't. It isn't saying, "It's okay," or "It doesn't hurt." I've heard pastors and Christians say, "If it still hurts, you haven't forgiven." That's bull. It will always make me angry that I was abused. It will always hurt. The difference now is that isn't what energizes me anymore.

Forgiveness never means that a person shouldn't be held accountable. Taking people to court, or facing whatever system there is to make them accountable, has nothing to do with forgiveness or unforgiveness. Forgiveness doesn't mean that I give them another chance to offend against me either. I don't believe it means I have to trust them again.

Forgiveness is freedom for me. When I was still not able to forgive, I constantly thought, "There's got to be a way to get even. I've got to take some kind of vengeance." But nothing will even the score. The ante can always be upped on the other side. The hard part is that the victim is the one who usually has to let it go. It's accepting that it's not fair.

Forgiveness does not always mean the relationship is restored, becasue I don't think it is possible sometimes. I get very angry with people who try to force reconciliation prematurely or with situations without safety nets. I think that's nuts. And I don't think forgiveness is done once. It's a process.

If my father or my uncle—well, my uncle is dead now—or my brothers were to repent, another level or dimension of forgiveness could happen. My dad is probably the one I have the hardest time forgiving. There are days I could rip his face off. He's a tiny little old man in a wheelchair who can't even speak anymore. Yet my heart still feels like it's holding its breath when I'm around him, when I see him. I go through times when the depth of pain is still pretty intense. But do I hate him? No, I don't. I look at him and I feel sad for him. He alienated himself from so many people that he sits alone in that home.

I don't need to be telling my story all the time or to a lot of people, but I needed someone to hear it, and I really searched long and hard for someone to hear it all.

I had times when it backfired on me. The first time I tried to talk I went to my pastor's wife who was a counselor. I was having flashbacks about a particular sort of repetitive thing with my brother. I started to tell her what I was remembering, and she began to quote scripture about there being things that are so profane that we don't talk about them. And so my translation was, "I'm profane. I'm evil. I'm dirty, and we don't talk about me." I was devastated. I tried again with another counselor, and that one wasn't much better. By the end of the second session he had me praying and raising my hands, confessing to being involved in immorality and wrong attitudes I had developed from it.

David is the first person who's been able to really listen to some of the things that I went through. I think he was the first person I really believed in my gut didn't feel any shame towards me. Being listened to and being believed were two enormous parts of my healing. And that sort of disempowered some of my history.

I didn't realize how important validation would be until I had it. I remember when Bryce, the police officer I reported this to, said to me, "Gayle, do you know that I believe you?" And I just stopped, and I said, "I'm not sure. Sometimes I think I'm crazy. Maybe I made it all up. Maybe I am crazy." And I asked, "Why do you believe

me?" And he was able to answer those questions for me. When I left there I felt like dancing.

I found it validating to hear those men in prison admit to their crimes and what they'd done. One man really struck me. He wanted me to tell him what his niece was going to face down the road. I talked to him about it, and it felt brutal. He said "No, I want to know what cost it is going to be to her."

I remember when I was talking with an offender about the guilt I felt about the rape and pregnancy. I was 15 years old; I wasn't a little tiny kid. Huge messages, tapes in my head, played this. He said, "Gayle, if I was your uncle or father, there is not one thing you could have done to have stopped me. Not one of my victims could have stopped me." Relief isn't even close to describing what I felt. It was different than hearing Bryce or David tell me it was not my fault. It was *huge* to hear offenders own that, to tell me that they were responsible and *wholly* responsible, that their victims had no part in it. To have people who had done the same kinds of things take responsibility was a sign to me that, "Yeah, there is hope."

The grace of God is something I'm beginning to search out and understand. Grace *for* me and *to* me. And for the people I met in prison. My belief in God and my relationship with God is so foundational, I don't see any meaning without it.

One of the battles I went through was with the Bible where it talks about how Jesus is touched by our feelings. I thought, "No, he wasn't a little girl in my home. He can't possibly know." Eventually I realized that it was at Calvary that he got it. That's where he bore not just my sin, but my pain, and he bore the offender's sin. He knew what it was like to be that offender, and he knew what it was like to be me.

That's when I began to trust that he could understand, that I could go to the Lord with this stuff. It was when he took on the mystery of the cross that he got it; that's when he knew. I wish I could put into words the depth of how that hit me.

This whole thing of restorative justice really grabs my heart. I want people to know that there's hope, that there's nothing too dark, nothing that has to be left in the darkness and hidden. I really want people to know that everything can be brought out. Hope is such a big word for me. I like words like *restoration*, for they speak to that.

And I like the word *transcendence*. It fits. I feel like I live in a totally other place than where I came from. My past is still part of me, and, as much as I wouldn't choose it again, I wouldn't trade it. I don't know how to reconcile those two thoughts, but I wouldn't be who I am without my past. And it's taken me a long time to get to where I am now.

— Gayle Macnab

# "What are you trying to tell me? What am I missing?"

I have very interactive communication with my higher power. When things happen, I usually wind up saying, "What are you trying to tell me? What am I missing?" I'm not reading the Burma Shave signs along the side of the road.

In 1991 my ex-husband showed up at my doorstep. When I told him to leave, he grabbed me and choked me until I couldn't talk. Then he stabbed me multiple times.

I was in the hospital for about four days, and I never lived in that place after that. I moved to this area immediately. Two of my friends went back with me to clean up all the blood. I was very angry that day. It was another mess of his that I had to clean up. There was a lot of cursing and crying that day.

I feel resentment that I was stripped from my home. I had lived there my whole life. I had a safety net that was so tight I could close my eyes and jump and be supported. I don't feel that

here. I'm an addictions counselor, and I had a thriving private practice that was gone in an instant because I had to move. I've had to come here and rebuild, and it's been a struggle. But some good things have happened, too.

I went to a shelter for abused women when I first moved here, and I was treated like a leper within that group. Now these were women that were abused, but they had never been stabbed. It was almost like I had the flu, like if they got too close to me they might catch it. There's nothing worse than being treated like a leper in a women's abuse group! I did go to AA meetings, and those people made me feel real comfortable. Now I don't care anymore. I figure, "Hey, it's my story. If my story scares you, that's not my problem."

I experienced a lot of shame. "You were a counselor. You should have known better. How could you let this happen to you?" Shame, shame. I don't care about that anymore, but I

ELIZABETH JACKSON

*Anybody who knows the Bible knows that God really treats his friends crappy sometimes. I mean, he leaves you wandering in the desert for 40 years; he puts you in a den of lions!*

should have listened to my gut. That's my message to others: If your gut says it's unsafe, pay attention to that.

I went through Catholic school so I majored in shame! But I really appreciate the training I was given there. I learned wonderful things—a structure, a faith to believe in, something that will see me through this stuff. When the attack was happening, I had a strong sense of good and evil battling in that room, God and Satan, if you want to call it that, two powerful forces. That's why I wasn't angry with God. It was because of God that I got out of there alive.

He got six to 15 years, and I'm fortunate he's still in. Right now I feel he's tucked in somewhere, and I'm somewhere else, and things are in place. I hate to live like this, but I know it's a real possibility he will try to do me additional harm. So the story hasn't ended.

I've been through many different traumas in my life. I never expected any of them to happen. I'm treading lightly because I don't want any more. That's why I get so terrorized when it comes toward parole time. It seems like for some reason I have been chosen for such things to happen to me! But, of course, anybody who knows the Bible knows that God really treats his friends crappy sometimes.

I used to hate it when people said, "Oh, you're so strong." To me being courageous and strong meant, "I can handle anything. Just give it to me." It meant having everything under control.

I found out that courage is walking through the door to come to therapy. Courage is getting up in the morning and going to work. Sometimes strength means being willing to become a basket case and letting other people support you. It means learning to be frail and fragile and vulnerable and allowing other people to see you in that state. That's courage! It's being able to say, "Could you be there for me?"

What have I learned about the meaning of life? I don't know. I'm still learning. You're gonna have to come round when I'm taking my last breath, and then I'll give you the clues, okay? I don't have enough data. Like I said, it's reading those signs along the roadside, waiting for the Burma Shave signs.

— Elizabeth Jackson

*I went to a shelter for abused women when I first moved here,*

*and I was treated like a leper in that group.*

*Now these were women that were abused,*

*but they had never been stabbed.*

*There's nothing worse than being treated like a leper*

*in a women's abuse group!*

# Part II
## *Looking for the Burma Shave Signs*
### Victimization and the Obligations of Justice

# Looking for the Burma Shave Signs—
## *Victimization and the Obligations of Justice*
### Howard Zehr

*Burma Shave signs were placed along highways in the United States from 1925 to 1963, when traffic was slower and lighter than it is today. A series of five small signs were attached to fence posts at intervals along the road, each showing one line of a four-part rhyme. The fifth sign usually read "Burma Shave," the name of the shaving cream company that sponsored the signs.*

*For those of us who were children during that era, a primary focus on a journey was looking for the "Burma Shave" signs. The meaning unveiled itself piecemeal; only with the fourth sign did the rhyme make sense.*

"Reading those signs along the roadside, waiting for the Burma Shave signs." Elizabeth Jackson's metaphor reflects a theme common to many of the survivors in this book: making a journey, looking for signs, attempting to make sense of what happened, and of life itself, searching for meaning that is only slowly and perhaps partially revealed.

The voices in the book have hinted at the pain and the tragedy which they have sought to transcend. I want to explore the contours of the journey—or journeys—that victims must make. What contribution should justice make to these passages? At the end, I offer some reflections on my own journey.

## A Whirlpool of Emotions

As these voices have reminded us, an encounter with violence is often a devastating experience that affects all areas of one's life. Penny Beerntsen characterizes it as a world knocked out of alignment, a logic destroyed. One victim has described his experience as "a profoundly political state in which the world has gone wrong, in which you feel isolated from the broader community by the inarticulable extremity of experience."[1] This expresses well the sense of disorder and isolation, the feeling of being out of control and cut off from others who have not shared a similar experience.

Victims of violence (as well as victims of many so-called "minor" crimes) experience an overwhelming range of strong emotions. Anger is often intense: anger at the one who did this, anger at oneself (self-blame is a normal response), anger at the "system," anger at friends who refuse to listen or who blame victims for what happened, anger at God who "allowed" this to happen. As is apparent from so many of the voices in this book, victims often undergo a religious crisis as they try to reassess their assumptions about a God who could allow or even cause this to happen.

Questions consume them: who did this? Why? Will they try it again? Survivors must also come to terms with their vulnerability and, sometimes, the question of why they survived when others did not. Fear is common, for themselves or others, and it may be associated with people or events—strangers, men, people of other races—for years to come.

Frightening, unsettling dreams may intrude. In their sleep victims may relive the crime, or they may take awful revenge on the offender. Either way, such dreams are unsettling. In addition, they may suffer unpredictable mood swings: between rage and the intolerance of rage; between intimacy and the fear of it; between repressing feelings and being overwhelmed by them. Awake or asleep, there is no escape from the memories and feelings. This can result in a further dimension of vulnerability, a perception that one's life is out of control.

A sense of isolation from others, even loved ones, is common as basic human relationships that were previously taken for granted are called into question. Along with this come many doubts, not only about relationships but about faith, meaning, even oneself. When victims' trauma is not acknowledged by others, or when their own interpretation of events are not respected, the doubts may extend to the validity of their feelings and their interpretations of the world.

Victims and survivors often undergo a profound process of grief: grief at the loss of loved ones, of one's sense of security and identity, loss of faith, loss of innocence. The fact of this grief, and the differing ways that marriage partners deal with grief, can lead to serious relational problems. Emma Jo and Herbert Snyder were not at all unusual in having to reassess their marriage. This is one reason that, among parents who have lost children to violence, divorce rates are high.

Oklahoma City bombing survivor Diane Leonard, asked to testify during Timothy McVeigh's sentencing trial, described the sense of grief in terms that echo some of the voices in this book: "I think the best way to describe it is I feel like I died, too, on April 19. I feel like my heart looks like that building. It has a huge hole that can never be mended . . . There is nothing in my life that is the same."[2]

What I have described here is often characteristic of a person who lives a "normal" life until violence intrudes. When a person experiences violence as normal, when that violence begins as a child, their whole world may be distorted, as Gayle Macnab and Janet Bakke suggest in their interviews.

## Pillars Undermined

The crisis of victimization is *comprehensive*. I often visualize it as three overlapping circles: a crisis of self-image (who am I really?), a crisis of meaning (what do I believe?), and a crisis of relationship (whom can I trust?). The crisis of victimization is also *fundamental* because it under- mines underlying assumptions or pillars upon which we build our sense of safety, wholeness, and identity. A number of such assumptions are important. Here I want to focus on three pillars which are especially basic: the assumptions of autonomy, order, and related-ness.[3]

All of us need to feel that we have substantial control over our own lives, or at least important parts of our lives. A work environment in which one is constantly ordered around by a superior authority feels dehumanizing and disrespectful. Slavery was dehumanizing for the same reason. Some people were in control of others, and this lack of personal power undermined a sense of wholeness. Likewise, at the time of a crime, someone takes control over the life of another, and this sense of being out of control continues as dreams and intense feelings continue to impose themselves. Such loss of control is deeply demoralizing and affects one's sense of safety, identity and well-being.

Each of us also needs the feeling of safety that is rooted in a sense of order. We need to believe that our world is basically orderly and that events can be explained. Cancer patients want to know why they have this disease, just as crime victims want to know why they were victimized. Answers restore order, and a sense of order is one of the pillars on which we base our lives. A world in which there is no discernible order feels unsafe and meaningless.

Parenthetically, these two pillars of autonomy and order help explain why victims so often blame themselves for what happened. To restore order, victims need to know why the crime happened. Absent real answers, blaming themselves is one way to provide a kind of answer. Also, blaming oneself is a way to achieve a sense of autonomy. If we attribute the crime to something we did, we feel some control because perhaps we can avoid that behavior in the future. If we are to blame, at least we are not helpless puppets.

The third pillar is relatedness. Healthy relationships with other people are essential for a sense of wholeness. We all need to be accepted by others. We need to know whom we can trust, where we fit in a web of relationships. Indeed, it is through interaction with others that we form and affirm our sense of identity.

Crime undercuts this sense of relatedness. Who did this? Who knows about this? Victims often become suspicious of strangers, even neighbors, who might be involved or who might be talking behind their backs. When family and friends do not respond as helpfully as they might—and many times we do not—victims often become alienated from them as well. Sometimes they feel that only another person who has been through a similar tragedy can understand. The web of relationships is distorted or destroyed.

Crime is deeply traumatic because it undercuts fundamental assumptions of autonomy, order, and relatedness. Violence depersonalizes, making those who were violated feel less than human. Victimization represents a profound crisis of identity and meaning, an attack on oneself as an autonomous but related individual in an orderly world.

Victims and survivors are often forced to revisit the same developmental issues that they had to resolve as they moved from childhood to adulthood—issues of identity, autonomy, self-control, social relationships. That occasions a deep grief process, not only for the person or things that actually may have been lost in the crime, but also for the part of themselves that has died, their trust in God and the world, their sense of place and identity. The sense of loss may be profound, and that in turn requires a difficult and often-resisted process of lament and mourning.

The experience of violence, then, calls into question our most fundamental assumptions about who we are, whom we can trust, and what kind of world we live in. The core trauma of victimization can be called the "three d's": disorder, disempowerment, disconnection. The movement from trauma to transcendence thus may mean revisiting issues we thought were long settled: order, empowerment, connection, identity. No wonder so many survivors speak of a journey, a journey made up of many components or sub-journeys. I want to explore several of these.

## Journey Toward Meaning

As the above implies, a key element in the trauma of violence is the destruction of meaning, and transcendence of trauma requires the re-creation of meaning. Some of the most powerful metaphors used by the people in this book reflect this process.

All of us construct our sense of identity and meaning by creating symbols of people, objects, and events, and preserving them in narratives—stories about who and what we are. When we are asked to say who we are, we usually tell a story. Our truths are embedded in our stories.

An experience of violence represents an attack on these narratives, an erosion of meaning, and therein lies a primary source of trauma.

To heal we have to recover our stories, but not just the old stories. We must create new or revised narratives that take into account the awful things that have happened. The suffering must become part of our stories. The re-creation of meaning requires the "re-storying" of our lives. Those who created the Truth and Reconciliation Commission of South Africa recognized that healing comes by facing one's past, coming to terms with it, drawing boundaries around it, incorporating experiences of hurt into a new story. To ignore or deny the pain can be deeply dysfunctional.

So to recover this sense of meaning it is important to express our pain. For many, that requires the repeated retelling of the narrative of violence. This retelling and venting allows us to ease the trauma and to begin to reconstruct a new narrative, to put boundaries around the story of suffering, to be victorious over it. Victimization is essentially an erosion of meaning and identity, so we must recover a redeeming narrative which reconstructs a sense of meaning and identity.

By telling our stories, we learn that we can face the pain without going insane. We make it part of our own story, a painful event in the larger narrative of our lives. This is why forgiving and forgetting do not belong in the same equation; if anything, it is "remember and forgive," as the Truth and Reconciliation Commission emphasized repeatedly. This "re-storying" process has a public as well as a private dimension. Judith Lewis Herman, in her seminal book *Trauma and Recovery*, prefers the term "testimony."[4] Stories are shaped in the telling and retelling, but they need compassionate listeners to hear and to validate their truths.

This journey toward meaning requires victims to make moral judgments about what happened and their responsibility in it. Like it or not, they often find themselves struggling to understand and explain what happened, in order to take an appropriate level of responsibility. Victims tend to blame themselves, taking far too much responsibility for what happened. For them, a key need is to be vindicated. This includes acknowledgment that a wrong was done to them and recognition that someone else is responsible, that they are not ultimately to blame. Yet as Herman has pointed out, most victims do not find it realistic to be totally absolved of all responsibility for what happened and/or how they responded to the trauma. Rather, the process of recovery requires locating an appropriate spot for themselves on the continuum between full responsibility and total denial of moral responsibility.

## Journey Toward Honor

As we work to "re-story" our lives, we not only create new meaning, but we begin to transform these stories of humiliation and shame into stories that include dignity and courage. Susan Russell explores this in her interview. It was in researching and writing about the heroic journey pattern that is found in the myths of so many cultures that she found her own identity as a heroic survivor and a way to move beyond shame. Oklahoma City bombing survivor Susan Urbach, on the witness stand during Timothy McVeigh's sentencing hearing, was asked by the prosecutor about the scar on her face. She answered like this:

"Well, it's my badge of honor . . . a scar, and any scar, tells a story . . . of a wounding and a healing that goes along with that wounding. And the more deeply you're wounded, the more healing that must come your way, that you must experience, for that wound to close up and for you to get that scar. I mean, you don't get your scar unless you've been wounded and you have healed. And I've got my scar."

Prosecutor: "So you're proud of your scar?"

"Yes."[5]

These examples suggest that the journey to meaning incorporates another journey—the journey toward honor and respect. That brings us to the topic of shame and its close cousin, humiliation.

Those of us who live in the western world are used to hearing the concepts of humiliation and honor applied to cultures and eras distant from our own. However, I am coming to believe that they continue to operate in powerful but often subterranean ways in the lives of both victims and offenders. Here I want to follow a hunch—that humiliation and honor provide an important lens for understanding the responses of victims.

The experience of shame and humiliation is a thread that runs through victims' experiences, and the struggle to remove or transform them is a central element in the journey to heal and belong. Why? One reason is that in western society, which values power and autonomy, it is shameful to be overpowered by others. When we are victimized, our status is lowered. We are humiliated by that event, but also often by the ways that we respond to that event—the things we did or didn't do at the time, the ways it affects us afterwards.

Shame is further heaped on us when our versions of what happened are not validated by others. The shame is compounded when we are forced to keep our experiences secret. In her interview, Ellen Halbert also ties the sense of shame felt by victims to the fingers of blame pointed by others, but also by oneself. Here we connect to what I expressed earlier: transcendence involves moral judgments set in stories of resilience, validated by others.

Whether we have victimized or been victimized, the journey from brokenness and isolation to transcendence and belonging requires us to re-narrate our stories so that they are no longer just about shame and humiliation, but are ultimately about dignity and triumph. Questions of meaning, honor, and responsibility are all part of this journey. Embedded in this is a desire for vindication.

## Journey Toward Vindication

William Ian Miller has argued that a sense of reciprocity is deeply imbedded in our psyches and cultures. We have an inherent drive to pay back what we owe and to be paid back what is owed to us, both the good and the evil. The exchange of gifts and the need to reciprocate honor and shame are closely related. "The failure to reciprocate," he says, "unless convincingly excused, draws down our accounts of esteem and self-esteem."[6] He goes on to show that honor and humiliation are ultimately tied to this concept of reciprocity. I would suggest that this need for reciprocity, for a righting of the balance of honor and humiliation, is tied to the need for vindication that many victims feel.

My work with victims suggests that the need for vindication is indeed one of the most basic needs that victims experience; it is one of the central demands that they make of a justice system. I'll go out a limb, in fact, and argue that this need for vindication is more basic and instinctual than the need for revenge. Revenge, rather, is but one among a number of ways that one can seek vindication.

When victims seek vindication from justice, they are in part seeking reciprocity through the removal of this shame and humiliation. By denouncing the wrong and establishing appropriate responsibility and restitution, the justice process can and should contribute to this.

## Journey to Justice

In short, crime represents a profound expression of disrespect for the victim as a person. Disrespect is depersonalizing. Crime is a denial of the personhood of the victim, a failure to value her or him as an individual. When we as friends or family members or caregivers fail to respect their needs, we perpetuate this disrespect for victims. When the legal system ignores victims, the cycle of disrespect is again perpetuated.

Although some of the people in this book had positive experiences with justice, victims often feel that the criminal justice process not only leaves them out, but steals their experience, reinterpreting it in foreign, legal terms. Often the offense is actually named something else when an offender pleads guilty in a plea agreement. If victims are involved at all it is often only in the role of witness. In that role, what they can contribute to the process is tightly circumscribed and emotionally very unsatisfying. Indeed, victims and survivors who were asked to be witnesses in the Timothy McVeigh Oklahoma City bombing trial had to go to Congress to be allowed into the court when they were not testifying.

The adversarial setting of the court is a hostile environment, an organized battlefield in which the strategies of aggressive argument and psychological attack replace the physical force of the medieval duel. "If you set out to design a system for provoking intrusive post-traumatic symptoms," Herman writes, "one could not do better than a court of law."[7] Is it any wonder that healing is so elusive?

On their journey for justice and healing, victims have many needs. While only they themselves can define their needs, and only they can address some areas of need, the larger community—including the justice process—has a major role to play in creating a context where healing is facilitated. Disempowerment and disconnection from others are the core of the trauma of victimization. Recovery, therefore, is based on empowerment and new connections, and this can only happen in relationship to others. Neither the community nor the justice process can replace the individual work that victims must do, but both can dramatically facilitate or impede the process of healing.

The focus of justice as we know it is not on victims' needs. But what if it were?[8] In the Christian and Jewish scriptures, the prophet Micah asks, "What does the Lord require?" and then the answer begins to unroll: "To do justice?" But another question is implied: What does justice require? What would it mean to do justice for victims? I want to suggest several areas of need that justice can and should address.

Most urgent, at least initially, is the creation of a *safe space*, emotionally as well as physically. Victims want to know that steps are being taken to prevent the recurrence of this experience, for them as well as for others. This includes a place to express, without judgment or blame, their anger and fears. It includes a place to mourn; mourning is a stepping-stone on the road to reordering.

Crime victims also often want some form of *restitution* or reparation. In part, this may be because they want repayment for losses, but more important often is the symbolic statement involved. Indeed, the actual losses are often impossible to compensate. Restitution—as well as apology—symbolizes a restoration of equity and implicitly states that someone else, not the victim, is responsible. It is a way of denouncing the wrong, absolving the victim, and saying who is responsible. Restitution, then, is about responsibility and meaning, as much as or more than it is about actual repayment of losses. Restitution is one form of validation and vindication, both of which are extremely important to most victims.

Also important are *answers* to questions. Victims want to know what happened and why, because, as noted above, answers restore the sense of order that is essential to health. They want answers that, to the extent possible, are real and not conjectured. They want answers that are as multi-layered as real life, not the simplistic, binary answers that emerge from the legal process. Some of these answers are interpretive and have to be discovered by victims themselves, for example, "Why did I react as I did? Why have I acted as I have since that time?" Other answers, however, are factual and must come from others: "What happened? Why

did it happen? What is being done about it?"

A fourth area of need has to do with what people who work with victims of domestic violence call "*truth-telling.*" As we have seen, victims need to tell their story, their "truth," perhaps over and over, to people who matter. It is in telling and retelling that all of us redefine our identities. Victims require the opportunity to vent their feelings of anger, betrayal, and grief. These are natural parts of the healing journey. Herman uses the language of "testimony" because it acknowledges that truth-telling has both individual and social, public and private, dimensions.

Finally, victims need to feel *empowered.* Power has been taken away from them. They need activities and experiences of involvement and empowerment.

## Restorative Justice

All justice processes involve rituals. Unfortunately, the rituals of the criminal justice process may serve certain needs of the state and the larger society, but they rarely serve victims well. A justice process oriented toward victims would incorporate their needs for rituals of lament, vindication, remembering, testimony, empowerment, re-connection.

Some of the survivors in this book have taken part in some form of restorative justice. Beginning in the late 1970s, but with roots in many historical traditions, restorative justice has developed in a number of countries as a way to reframe our assumptions and approaches to justice. Today there are restorative justice programs operating in most states and provinces of the U.S. and Canada. While many are aimed at dealing with less violent crimes, increasingly, programs are being devised for crimes of severe violence.

Restorative justice programs have emerged above all as an attempt to address the needs of those affected by crime—communities and offenders, but especially victims. In doing so, they seek to provide a context where victims' needs for safety, restitution, answers, truth-telling, and empowerment can be addressed.

The best known restorative justice programs offer victims a carefully facilitated encounter—direct or indirect—with the offender in their case, or with other similar offenders. Such encounters must be entirely the free choice of the victim or survivor. Sometimes the name "victim-offender mediation" is used to describe such encounters, but "mediation" is actually a problematic term in this field, and especially when applied to crimes of severe violence. Some use the term "facilitated dialogue," or victim offender "conferencing," for this approach.

Restorative justice does not always involve encounters, however. Indeed, there are a whole range of approaches within the field. Moreover, restorative justice is essentially not a program or programs. It is, rather, a philosophy of justice based on two fundamental principles: that crime is essentially harm, and that all of the real stakeholders ought to be engaged in the response to a crime. A program of encounter is only one way to implement these principles.

The modern legal system focuses on the breaking of laws instead of the actual harm that is done. In fact, legally, the real victim—as Bion Dolman says so eloquently—is not the person violated but the state. Consequently, the real victim has only secondary standing in the process, and her or his needs may be neglected or ignored. The focus of justice is on making sure the offender gets what he or she deserves, not on addressing the victim's needs.

Restorative justice, in contrast, says that what really matters about crime is that harm has been done to people and their relationships. Once that is acknowledged, two cardinal principles emerge. First, the ones harmed—victims and survivors—should be central to justice. The starting point for justice, in other words, would be the needs of victims, as the victims themselves define them. Second, the question of offender accountability should focus on encouraging offenders to understand and, to the extent possible, take responsibility for that harm.

The legal system has the government doing justice "to" the offender in the name of victim and community, but without much space for the latters' voices and roles. Restorative justice argues that victims and communities, along with offenders, are key stakeholders in justice and, to the extent possible, they should be engaged in determining the outcome of justice. They should have as much information about each other and the event as possible, and they should be involved as much as possible. While it is not always appropriate or desired, one option that should be open is for victims to have an opportunity to confront and dialogue with perpetrators. In cases of severe violence, such programs rarely are designed to impact the legal outcome of the case, but they do offer substantial benefits for victims and offenders who participate. A number of the people in this book have been through such a process.

In short, restorative justice reminds us that we cannot "do justice" without concern for all parties—victims, as well as offenders and communities.

## My Own Journey

I have never been the victim of a serious crime. In fact, during my early days of criminal justice involvement I knew very few victims and, to be honest, didn't want to know them. I was primarily concerned about the well-being of offenders, and I didn't see the need to understand the "other side." As I then understood it, justice for offenders could be sought without much reference to victims. Besides, empathizing with victims would only confuse the issue emotionally, making it harder for me to advocate for offenders. These feelings are a natural consequence of the adversarial framework of our justice system. Both victim advocates and offender advocates often believe that it is not necessary to understand the other side and fear that to understand would make their work more difficult.

In the late '70s I left Alabama, where I was teaching and practicing, and moved to Elkhart, Indiana, where I became director of what was then called the "victim offender reconciliation program," the first such program in the United States. I began writing the how-to manuals that allowed this first effort to be duplicated elsewhere. Eventually, this program became a primary model for victim-offender conferencing programs throughout the world. I spent considerable time consulting with and training persons in communities who wanted to start such programs. Initially the approach grew out of experience and instinct more than theory. It was only later that we developed the conceptual framework and language of "restorative justice" that has gained currency today.

Victim-offender encounters forced me for the first time to interact with victims. As I began to listen to their voices, to hear them express their needs and perspectives, my assumptions about justice began to reel. As I listened to victims, whether they chose to meet with their offender or not, I began to sense their pain and to understand their perspectives. No longer did I believe that justice for offenders could be pursued without involving victims or addressing their needs. In fact, I became convinced that victims must be central in the search for justice. Victims must be key stakeholders rather than footnotes in the justice process. In a book first published in 1990, I argued that what was needed was something more fundamental than a few new programs for victims or offenders. In *Changing Lenses*, I called for a restorative "lens" or vision of justice.[9]

I recognized even then that the language of "restoration" was problematic. How can one restore a murdered child, for instance? On the other side, many offenders need not to be restored, but to be transformed. However, the term "restoration" did capture something of the relational and needs-oriented dimension of what justice should be. The word's popularity today suggests that it does connect with something deep and intuitive for many people.

Over the years, a variety of experiences have taken me deeper into the world of victims. In addition to working with victims of violent crimes, I have listened to victims of massacre, genocide, terrorism, and repression in other parts of the world, such as Northern Ireland, southern Sudan, Central America, and South Africa. While the circumstances and some of the specific needs may be different, I have heard many common themes. I am much more aware of victims' experiences than I once was, much more able to live with and affirm the intense and contradictory feelings of victims, much more able to honor their perspectives, even when circumstances call upon me to work with other participants in the justice process. In all I do, I aspire to be a victim advocate.

But I have yet another confession to make. It has taken me longer to "get it" than I'd like to admit. The drawn-out process of my "conversion" may be symptomatic of others' journeys.

As I began to work with victims, my "lenses" changed. I spoke of the importance of victims' perspectives and involvement in justice, and I believed it. Yet, as I look back, I realize that I still thought I knew what was best for victims. I assumed we could begin programs, later invite victims in to help support and run our programs, and, when they didn't jump at the

chance, could say we tried. I realize now that I was afraid of the difficult dialogue that would be inevitable. I acknowledge now that I wanted to minimize the ambiguities, paradoxes, and contradictions that are the stuff of real life.

I can't date my conversion, but today I have a conviction that the involvement of victims and victim advocates must be a precondition for anything called justice. Moreover, those of us who have not been victims have a responsibility to fine-tune our own sensitivities to victim issues so that we can share responsibility for monitoring their issues.

People of color should not have to carry the full burden of monitoring and calling attention to the operation of race and privilege in our society. Those of us of European ancestry have a responsibility to become aware of the privilege that we have inherited and to speak out. Nor should women have to be the only voices to speak out on gender issues. In the same way, victims and survivors should not have to carry their burdens alone.

What does justice require? Restorative justice suggests that we need to change our lenses, and this in turn requires us to change our questions. Justice for victims will not be served if we maintain our primary focus on the old questions that drive our justice system: What laws have been broken? Who did it? What do they deserve?

Real justice requires that we start with victims. Who has been hurt? What do they need? Whose obligations and responsibilities are they? Who are the primary "stakeholders," and how can they best be involved? Only when we allow such questions to frame our quest for justice will victims attain the place they deserve.

This book is not an effort to promote restorative justice programs, but it does reflect a key restorative justice principle: that victims' voices should be heard, in all their diversity and complexity, even when they are difficult to hear, even when we are uncomfortable with their positions. We need to hear these voices if we are to have a real dialogue about crime and justice. We need to hear these voices if we are to do justice.

[1] Bruce Shappiro, "One Violent Crime," *The Nation*, 3 April 1995, pp. 444-452.

[2] Quoted in *NOVA Newsletter*, 17/2 (1997), 2.

[3] See, for example, Robert Johnson, *Death Work: A Study of the Modern Execution Process* (Pacific Grove, CA: Brooks/Cole Publishing, 1990), 128-130.

[4] Judith Lewis Herman, *Trauma and Recovery: The Aftermath of Violence—From Domestic Abuse to Political Terror* (New York, New York: Basic Books, 1992). This essay draws upon Herman's important book at a number of points.

[5] Quoted in *NOVA Newsletter*, 17/2 (1997), 3.

[6] William Ian Miller, *Humiliation* (Ithaca, New York: Cornell University Press, 1993).

[7] Herman, p. 72.

[8] Susan Herman, Executive Director of the National Center for Victims of Crime, has, in fact, advocated a separate, parallel system of justice for victims.

[9] *Changing Lenses: A New Focus for Crime and Justice* (Scottdale, PA: Herald Press, 1990/95).

# National Resource Organizations for Victim Issues

*The following is a select list of national resource organizations. In addition to providing resources, these organizations' literature and websites provide links to many other national, state, and provincial victim organizations in the United States and Canada.*

**National Center for Victims of Crime (NCVC)**
2111 Wilson Boulevard, Suite 300
Arlington, VA 22201
Phone: 703-276-2880
800-FYI-CALL Helpline
www.ncvc.org

**National Organization for Victim Assistance (NOVA)**
1730 Park Road, NW
Washington, DC 20010
Phone: 202-232-6682
Email: nova@try-nova.org
www.try-nova.org

**Office for Victims of Crime (OVC)**
Box 6000
Rockville, MD 20849-6000
Phone: 800-627-6872

http://www.ojp.usdoj.gov/ovc/
**National Coalition Against Domestic Violence**
Rita Smith, Executive Director
1201 East Colfax Avenue, Suite 385
PO Box 18749
Denver, CO 80218-0749
Phone: 303-839-1852
www.ncadv.org/

**National Sexual Assault Resource Center**
123 North Enola Drive
Enola, PA 17025
Phone: 717-909-0710

**Canadian Resource Center for Victims of Crime**
100-141, rue Catherine Street
Ottawa, Ontario K2P 1C3, Canada
Phone: 613-233-7614
www.crcvc.ca

# Acknowledgments

A project like this is inevitably a collaboration. I am grateful to those who helped to connect me with the people in this book: Dave Gustafson, Sandy Bergen, Ellen Halbert, George Donnelly, Wilma Derksen, Kathy Buckley, Missy King, Marcia Drew, David Doerfler and Bruce Kittle were especially helpful. I am also thankful for feedback on the text from Cheryl Guidry Tyiska, Director of Victim Services for the National Organization of Victim Assistance (NOVA). The suggestions of my editor, Phyllis Good, have been invaluable. Those who painstakingly transcribed the tapes—Elaine Zook Barge, Jean Gerber, Barb Toews Shenk, Marisol Cruz—played a key role. Ruby Friesen Zehr—my most important source of support and critique over almost 35 years of marriage—made many helpful suggestions, some solicited, some not.

Two people have been especially important. Mary Achilles, the governor's victim advocate for the Commonwealth of Pennsylvania, has played a dual role: her enthusiasm and support for the project have keep me going throughout and her candid feedback has helped to keep me accountable to the victim community. Tammy Krause—once my student, now my colleague—has provided much encouragement and feedback as well. Her artistic intuition, sense of story, and concern for integrity have been extremely helpful. Without the support of these two, this would be a quite different book.

Major funding for the research came from a grant provided by the Open Society Institute's Center on Crime, Communities and Culture; this was part of a larger "Listening Project" grant designed to allow the victim services community to express their concerns and ideas about the restorative justice field. Additional support was provided by the Schowalter Foundation through Mennonite Central Committee (MCC) U.S.; I am thankful for the help of Lorraine Stutzman Amstutz, Director of the MCC Office on Crime and Justice, for her assistance in this. Eastern Mennonite University provided release time from teaching to work on this project.

Although I get credit as author of this book, the real authors are those who have allowed their words and photographs to be presented. I am deeply grateful to each person included in this book and also to those who, because of limitations of space, were interviewed but not included here. Their reflections, their trust, their collaboration have been real gifts.

— Howard Zehr

# About the Photography

The photographs were made with a Hasselblad 500C/M using a 150 mm lens and occasionally an 80 mm lens.

Film was Fuji's Neopan 400, developed in D-76 1:1.

Photos were printed on Ilford's Multigrade Warmtone RC, using a customized Omega enlarger and color head and Schneider Componon-S lens.

Lighting was provided by a White Lightning Ultra 600 in a Westcott Halo Light Modifier and occasionally a reflector.

The collapsible backdrop was repainted for me by my colleague Scott Jost.

— Howard Zehr

---

## If you would like to order this book in quantities . . .

If your support group, reading group, book discussion group, or any other group would like to order 6 or more copies of this book at a discount, call Good Books at 800/762-7171. Or send an email to Good Books at custserv@goodbks.com, requesting a discount schedule. *Transcending: Reflections of Crime Victims* is a thoughtful book for group discussion.

For single copies, please support your local bookstore. The book is also available on our website at www.goodbks.com.

Photo by Ingrid DeSanctis

# About the Author and Photographer

Dr. Howard Zehr is an internationally known practitioner, writer, lecturer, and teacher in the field of criminal justice. He is considered one of the founders of the contemporary restorative justice movement. His groundbreaking book, *Changing Lenses: A New Focus for Crime and Justice*, is widely regarded as a standard in the field.

The author was one of the early pioneers in victim-offender mediation and continues to be involved in this and related work. One of his primary areas of concern is the role of victims in justice, and especially in restorative justice programs. He and a colleague were appointed by the federal court in the Timothy McVeigh Oklahoma City bombing trial to assist attorneys in working with victims. Out of this developed a program of exchange visits of survivors from the U.S. embassy bombing in Nairobi, Kenya and the bombing of the federal building in Oklahoma City. Another outcome is an ongoing initiative to sensitize defense attorneys to victims' perspectives and to incorporate survivors' voices in death penalty cases.

Dr. Zehr has lectured, consulted, and trained in several dozen countries throughout the world. He has worked with community groups, police, and correctional agencies in many countries, including Northern Ireland, England, Russia, Jamaica, Bosnia, New Zealand, and South Africa.

He is also an accomplished documentary and journalistic photographer. He has worked professionally as a photojournalist, photographing in some 20 countries, and has conducted numerous photo-interview projects. Publications include the book *Doing Life: Reflections of Men and Women Serving Life Sentences* (Good Books, 1996).

After serving 19 years as director of the national criminal justice office of Mennonite Central Committee, an international humanitarian organization, in 1996 Dr. Zehr joined the faculty of the Conflict Transformation Program of Eastern Mennonite University in Harrisonburg, Virginia. This is an international graduate program emphasizing value-based practice in the areas of conflict transformation and restorative justice and provides a base for ongoing practice as well as teaching.

Zehr received his B.A. from Morehouse College (the first white graduate of this historically African American college), his M.A. from the University of Chicago, and his Ph.D. from Rutgers University. He is married to Ruby Friesen Zehr and has two daughters and two grandchildren.